Stripped
Windows

Héctor del Valle

To order additional copies of this book, contact:
Xlibris
844-714-8691
www.Xlibris.com
Orders@Xlibris.com

ISBN: Softcover   978-1-6698-2033-8
        EBook   978-1-6698-2032-1

Print information available on the last page

Rev. date: 04/20/2022

CONTENTS

My Family: Daribel, Myrna, Hector Jr.

DEDICATION

I never thought that writing a book was so difficult. I was always willing to leave something tangible for my children to enjoy: money, a house, a car, pictures, or collectibles.

However, overtime, and as my retirement was approaching, I could reflect in such a way that I decided to leave verbatim writings of some meaningful details that marked my life as a son, as a brother, neighbor, student, professor, and as a serviceman.

During these facets, my life was being shaped while the last born child of Monche and Tunila, my loving parents, kept growing. That is how I became *"el regalón," "el Benjamín"* of the family, the child with a babyface, *"etomilié,"* as my grandmother Eufemia used to call me, "Gamaliel," as my sister Virginia's husband Chito, called me, *"ejtol,"* as my brothers and sisters called me, "deval," by those who did not speak Spanish, or "del Valle," by my colleagues.

From the regalón and a *"fajardeña,"* two adorable children were born whom I love with all my heart: Daribel and Héctor Jr. (Titon). For them, although they grew up in a different environment, I wish they had better experiences than those I had while I was growing physically and intellectually. I wish them a prosperous and healthy life, so they may evolve in the society they have to live in.

To you, Titon and Dari, my two loved ones, my two "diamonds," my two "treasures," my two blessings, I dedicate this book and I pass on to you a legacy that will not be repeated in this life or any other person. A legacy that you both, as well as those who read my book, will be able to ponder, to judge, to evaluate, to enjoy.

This literary legacy will recount some insights without "curtains" that may limit the harsh reality without fearing what people may say.

Enjoy it and keep it in such a way that you may share it with my grandchildren, great-grandchildren, and great-great-grandchildren.

Simplemente,

Papi

PROLOGUE

Mata de plátano, a ti,
A ti te debo la mancha
Que ni el jabón ni la plancha
Quitan de encima de mí.
Desque jíbaro nací
Al aire llevo el tesoro
De tu racimo de oro
Y tu hoja verde y ancha:
Llevaré siempre la mancha
Per secula seculorum

Luis Lloréns Torres

Plantain tree,
I owe you the stain,
that neither the soap nor the iron
can take away from me.
Since I was born *"jibaro"*
In the air, I carry the treasure
of your golden bunch of bananas
and your wide green leaf.
I will always carry your stain
eternally

I feel proud of my humble roots. I will never deny where I was born, not in a hospital surrounded by machines, doctors, nurses, white sheets and pillows, but in a simple house made of wood and zinc, assisted by a *"comadrona"* with coarse hands who laid me on a white canvas hammock hanging with ropes and tied up to the corners of the living room. There was the last moaning begotten child of the family. There was my tiny swinging body while in the home's yard, the tender plantain trees were also growing and swinging their greenish wide leaves with a voluptuous rhythm and offering me a welcoming to the rural world. They were also ready to give birth bunches of plantains for the nutrition of the newborn child. They were going to place on me the royal blood stamp of Africa, of Spain, and the Tainos: the plantain stain. Both the native *reinita* and the *ruiseñor* were singing their best songs from a nearby mango tree as a tribute to the newborn. The famous *pitirre was* at the top of the green royal palm "antenna" while watching for the enemy: the native hawk. The *guamá,* árbol *Madre,* was tenderly casting its warm shadows over the coffee trees, which were already showing its coral red beans and getting ready to offer them to be picked by the hands of the family. They were going to be dried while being exposed to the heat of the sun in the *batey,* toasted in the *cazuela,* ground in the *molinillo,* and served as a daily breakfast drink called *café.* The newborn as a grown-up child, as well as the rest of the family members, were going to taste the aromatic fresh brewed coffee from an empty can that was prepared for that purpose.

My story has windows,
Some are small,
some are open,
Others, semi open,
Some are sealed,
And only the pain
of the author
feels them,
smells them,
hears them,
opens them
by pressing.

Windows that have been super closed,
that others think they never existed,
That they can not conceive them.
but they exist,
and they existed,
making idiosyncrasies,
marking paths, small paths, long paths, dark paths,
footpaths, secret shortcuts.

I was told not to get through them,
but at the persistence
of my conscience,
the windows have talked to me.
They have screamed at me
what I never said,
what the subconscious mind
was suppressing,
and compressing.

And here starts
the truth of my story
through some windows,
and I do not want to suppress them,
or close them,
and I do not want to hide them.
I want to open them
and look through them
without restraints.
I want to go across them
unhurriedly, assertively, elaborately
even if I had to pay a price,
or if it hurts me,
although when I went through them
the voice of those who have windows was heard
Because they decorate them,
they polish them,
They paint them,
they clean them, they change them,
to hide the forbidden,
the dark side of their story,
the unknown,
the hidden for fear,
what distresses them,
what they burry,
in the cemetery of pain,
in the scarcity niche,
and the social verdict.

Here are the windows of my story,
so you may go through them with me
fearless, without prejudice,

without mockeries or blames,
so you may slowly look,
listen, smell, taste, and even touch
occasions of anguish, frustrations,
enthusiasm, admiration,
precocities, rejections,
achievements.

Here are the stripped windows of my life.
Windows that I open to express
memories of loneliness,
weakness,
temptations,
reflections.
Memories that pullulate my mind,
like bees in the honeycomb,
as nightmares,
as dreams,
sad experiences,
full of anguish,
full of insecurities,
memories of pain,
memories of anxiety.
Six windows before you,
From me,
To you.

The First Family House

Chapter 1

THE LIGHT OF A BARRIO SAW ME BORN WHILE TUNILA WAS PUSHING OUT HER "REGALÓN"

Memories from my childhood are vague. My parents had their thirteen children in *Barrio* Mariana, in the Gray City of Humacao. I had the opportunity to closely see the mountain where the family hut made of wood and zinc was built.

My middle name was part of my name until I was approaching my eighteenth birthday. At that age, my father started to collect Social Security benefits and my birth certificate was necessary to receive part of this benefit as a minor. Surprisingly, my middle name was not officially registered and I could not use it anymore as my mother informed me. Later, I was told that two more children died at an early age, a boy and a girl. The boy's name was Gamaliel. My mother wanted to honor the dead boy by giving me the same name.

According to Mami, when I was a newborn, my older sister, Virginia, was swinging the hammock where I was sleeping.

—Mami! There is a rope hanging from the hammock!—shouted Alicia.

—A rope?

—Yes, Mami, look at it!

My mother could not wait and she carefully approached the hammock.

—That is not a rope, it is a snake!

Suddenly, and impulsed by her maternal instinct, and like a real heroine protecting her newborn without thinking about it, she boldly grabbed the snake and swung it up in the air before throwing it far away.

As time passed, the family moved to *Barrio* Tejas and we were hosted by my sister Virginia's in-laws. Here we open a little and tender window through which we can see Monche and Tunila's *"regalón"* getting up at five o'clock in the morning waking up all members of the family while he was singing the *corito* that follows:

> "There is a fire that I want
> To light it up in my heart
> The fire of God is so holy
> That it embraces us in the same heat."

Where and from whom did I learn it? I do not know, but I can imagine it was from my mother who used to take me to church since I was a child. This morning awakening was mentioned by my family as a joke until I became a young guy.

Later, my father decided to move to another area of the same *barrio*. From this move I remember seeing my father building a house with wood and zinc like an inverted "v". This one was our residence for many years until a new solid concrete house was built in the *terraplén,* as we used to call the plateau prepared by the dozer that was used to pave the road connecting the city with the *barrio.*

Let's talk about Papi, my father, about *Don Monche* as he was known in the neighborhood. His father's name was Gregorio or Don Goyo. He lived with my grandmother Laureana one hectometre (one hundred meters) away from my house. These units of length were white pieces of concrete partly buried at the sides of the road to indicate the distance between the city and the *barrio.*

There was not a big physical resemblance between my father and his father. My grandfather was tall, slender, and well-shaped. His abundant white mustache gave him an aristocratic look. Although he was a peasant, I remember that his hands were not designed for gross force works. I believe that my hands are a duplicate of his hands or my mother's hands.

Don Goyo executed his barber's trade in a very good manner. On many occasions, I was immersed in watching while he gave Papi a haircut in the living room. He used to place a big white cloth on my father who was subjected to the careful and detailed haircut and his shaving process from his progenitor. Everything happened amid a silence which was interrupted by my grandmother calling the chickens to eat the corn that she used to throw at the *batey* using one single syllable a few times.

—Pi, pi, pi, pi, pi!...

—Where have all the chickens gone?—she asked herself when they did not come quickly. Later, all the hens, chickens, and roosters approached the front of the house to have a dry corn feast.

The most interesting moment happened when Don Goyo finished shaving Papi's beard.

He used to apply enough of a lotion called *Brisas del Caribe* which probably had a high concentration of alcohol because Papi was shaking from head to toe at the contact of the liquid with the small cuts made by the razor. I laughed at this climax considering it a great spectacle.

Papi was smaller than his father. He had a high-intensity nose with wide-open nostrils. His big black eyes seemed to cover the whole scene at a 180-degree angle. This physical feature was rejected by Mami when Papi made some loving approaches trying to conquer her when she was only fifteen.

—I will never marry that big-eyed guy!—she used to say with much dislike. But the big-eyed guy overcame it.

Papi's big and rude hands were dedicated to driving a number eight locomotive from the sugar cane industry. It was from the *Central Ejemplo,* which does not exist anymore. It was located in *El Pueblito de los Perros.* I walked through this place to bring Papi's dinner, *almojábanas* en *fiambreras,* but I never saw so many dogs.

Papi used to get up at four o'clock in the morning to travel to work. During those days I used to sleep on a white hammock made of canvas in the living room. Papi woke me up at five to give me a can full of coffee that he made himself. This childhood window was stamped on my memory as a loving paternal act. We may remember our parents' mistakes, bad behaviors, addictions, rejections, and many other unpleasant moments, but when we talk about those moments that they show care, affection, and love for their children, those experiences will be remembered forever so we can forgive and forget disillusions.

Papi was the only one supporting the family financially while Mami was dedicated to raising the children at home. The money Papi made from the sugar cane factory was not enough, but we had a food reserve from the farm: yams, sweet potatoes, green beans, rice, bananas, plantains, breadfruits, and avocados among others. We also raised chicken for meat and eggs, and we had a cow for the milk. Her name was *Ojinegra,* for her big black eyes. She was a very meek cow like the one from the story *Adiós Cordera* written by Rubén Darío.

Many times I took her back to the farm after having her milked and I addressed her using apostrophic language.

—You are our cow. Although you can not talk to me, with your "Muuu" you seem to tell me your answers. You never argue when we take you out of your farm full of grass, cohiter, and other plants you like to eat for your food and then you lay down ruminating the grass you swallowed during the day. You never protest while being pulled by a rope. It was like saying: "you must follow us to our house where we tie you up to a pole restraining your bovine freedom." Stoically you stay resisting your immobility until someone comes to tie up your back legs supposedly for avoiding your kicks while being milked. They ignored that your main virtue was being meek. Then, they bring your young calf so he may suck your udder where you store the white liquid we call milk, but as the calf opens his mouth taking one of your tits to feed himself, the person in charge of milking sticks his hand inside the calf's mouth to withdraw him so he can not drink the whole milk. Once your udder is swollen with plenty of milk, they tighten each tit one by one to get the calcium-rich liquid. You listen when the stream of milk gets in contact with the metal container and you wish all this milk were for your offspring. But you do not say anything, not even Muuuuuu! And I keep looking at your face while being *ñangotao* in front of you. And you look at me with your intense black amber eyes. I believe that with that look you are telling me about your frustration.

Ojinegra, today I return you to your territory, to your habitat where you can be free of the rope that tight your neck, of the other rope that was on your legs, and of the squeezes of your tits. I return you to the enclosure where you can choose your favorite grass, to the stream where you lick the water that relieves your thirst caused by the heat of the day, to the shadows of mangos, fruit bread, and avocado trees. Far away, you can see that your offspring was taken away from you until the next day, but you accept it. You only say, Muuuuuuu!

At night you lay down on your side and start to ruminate. You would like to be a different being in the animal kingdom. One that does not have to be domestic like you are. To be a lion, an elephant, a tiger, but then, you change your mind and you accept yourself as you are: a cow. A family beloved cow. You feel proud belonging to a family that receives from you. A family that will grow and change for many years, even if your lifespan would be between fifteen and twenty-five years. And you look happy when you see me coming to get you. And you walk behind me saying your Muuu! And I turn my head and I answer —*Muuuchas gracias,* Ojinegra!

On many occasions, Papi came home in the afternoon with some pieces of BH sugar cane sticks (this is how they used to call it). He said that this kind was the best and the sweetest. I agreed as I peeled a piece exposing the white fibrous pulp and took it into my mouth to suck into it and to swallow the pure juice. Great experience when the sugar cane treated me with the rich and abundant amount of its sweetest nectar.

There was a gloomy day full of uncertainty for the family. This happened at the end of the *zafra* and the beginning of the *tiempo muerto* as mentioned by *Manuel Méndez Ballester* in his book. On that evening, Papi used to bring more sugar cane sticks than usual. He also brought the black thick syrup, but he also had an unhappy face and a sad soul. Later, around five o'clock, we could hear the crying noise of a siren coming from the *Central* as it was mourning like saying:

—The *zafra* came to an end!

The Rivera family had a house across the road: Ignacio (Chilí), Manuela, Goyo, Isabel, William, and Felo were the family members. The last two were my childhood buddies, especially William. With him, I studied in the same school. With him, I climbed the mango, *mamey, and tamarindo* trees. With William, I looked for ripe guavas cutting them in two halves avoiding the experience of swallowing a worm. With William I looked for *pajuiles, cerezas, jácanas, maricaos.*

One day I climbed a sweet lemon tree and I did not realize that there was a wasp nest. I got multiple stings and my whole face was swollen like a ham, and I did not bring home any lemon.

With William, Felo, Rubén, Juan, Cusin, and Cleto, I bathed in the river, especially when its waters were flooded, for that time many wide deep ponds were formed and we enjoyed swimming in them being naked.

The river was about half an hour's walk from our house. We had to go across two farms and a narrow stream. When we arrived, we went down a path that led to a grayish rock. We used it to get naked leaving our clothes on it. Above, there was like a sphere of bamboo trees reacting to the soft breeze with a peaceful and tender hiss while caressing each other. It was a very special and unique experience being submerged in the water, feeling the tickles of the sand under our feet, listening to the timed noise of the trees, and the boys screaming when they got in contact with the cold water.

Life in the countryside, with all its purity, all its naivety, all its peace, and humbleness, offered us the opportunity for barefoot walking, to go outdoors to the *batey* on a rainy day, to let the rain caress us with its multiple and pure liquid crystals, to let the *agua de tiempo* as we called it, to slide easily over our infant faces covered with the *bembeteo* sugar, the residuals of the ripe mango, the dribbled mix of *gofio,* and the oily *pegao.* And we jumped with excitement, we danced freely, dipping our tiny feet into the mud. Child and nature fused into a dance. We used to lay down on the grass facing up the sky so we could locate the constellations: the Three Kings, the Three Marys, the Little Eyes of Saint Lucie. We also pointed at the stars with our fingers challenging the superstition that stated it was a bad omen.

At the beginning of February, we celebrated the famous *candelarias* in Puerto Rico. It was a whole spectacle in our neighborhoods. We did not know its meaning, but we united for the celebration. We bunched the wood and many dry leaves together to light them up and walked around the fire. The heavy darkness around made the fires blaze with a matchless show. The air got permeated with the smell of smoke and burning wood and leaves. The scope of the *batey* was full of the noise from the burning leaves and our screams saying…

—Long live the *candelarias*! Long live!

Children from the city do not experience this celebration, since they are surrounded by asphalt, high buildings, and cars. The city is an urban neighborhood with many limitations. Starry nights are not enjoyed by the presence of so many artificial lights. The majority of the trees do not bear fruits, they are mainly ornamentals.

Our house was located on a high plateau, different from the rest of the neighborhoods. From this location, we could see a wide range of all the mountains around the *Ciudad Gris* as they called the city of Humacao. A good section of the El *Yunque* mountains can be seen on the left side. They had a bluish color. From that point, there were a series of mountains, some high, others low that ended in a vast valley in front of the Caribbean Sea which proudly exhibits the island of Vieques. To the right, there was another section of mountains with a flowing silhouette within an abundant mark of green on its pine trees safeguarding the *barrios* of Buena Vista, Candelero, and Mariana.

Some days, far from my house, I could see the crowds of people carrying a coffin and heading to the cemetery. They protected themselves from the sun with umbrellas that looked like mushrooms in movements.

Some families could not bear the costs of a funeral home facility and decided to have the wake in their own homes. A person who knew the embalming process was called to preserve the corpse until the next day. I was looking at how that person was introducing a liquid through the nose of the dead one and placing a big metal bowl full of ice under the coffin. After that, everybody was waiting for the hot chocolate and the soda crackers that were served at midnight.

The next day the funeral procession departed the house with four men carrying the coffin upon their shoulders and heading to the city. If the dead were evangelical, there was a group singing,

"When the Roll is Called Up Yonder"

At the cemetery, we never missed the frenetic reactions of the family with some peculiar expressions like,

"Why did you leave us?"

"Take me with you!"

Another scene that I was able to see was when transporting a sick person to the hospital. They carried them on a hammock which was tied to both ends of a pole from the agave plant. All this was done showing the commitment that the countrymen had in terms of empathy with their neighbors.

There was a *comadrona* in the neighborhood that was always available to assist mothers in labor. Her name was Doña Lola. She was Abelardo's mother who became an evangelical pastor for the neighborhood. Later, he moved to New York City and was in charge of a big famous church known as

La Sinagoga in Manhattan. When Doña Lola arrived at the house, all the doors were shut and we could not get close. We could hear the screaming of the mother giving birth. We also saw when the father was passing wet hot towels to the *comadrona*.

Not far from my house, there was a lush green mango tree that was very easy to climb. Its wide trunk had reachable branches allowing us to explore so many hideouts. Climbing this *mango tino*, as we named it, was a whole adventure. We could grab the fruits with our own hands and then enjoy the sweetness of fresh and juicy mango. Besides that, being up there, we could feel the strong force of winds swinging us like being on a hammock. It was like a complete merge between the wind and the tree on a perfect maternal character.

I felt profoundly sad when I saw this tree fall under the wrath of a storm in August. 1956. I remember that when it was announced that Santa Clara, (this was the name of the tropical disturbance,) was going to land in Puerto Rico, we started to make preparations for what we as kids considered to be a great event. It was informed by the authorities that the eye of the storm was going to make landfall through the city of Patillas. Humacao, where I used to live, was not far from there.

Papi, as a whole carpenter, had built a *tormentera* not far from our house. It was located next to our neighbor farm's border. Papi dug deep enough to make a square hole on a hill with concrete walls. He installed a very strong roof at almost ground level. It looked like a partially buried building. This would make it very safe against any storm or hurricane. It had only one door. It also had a small window facing the East and a pipe-shaped opening on the opposite side to keep the air pressure during the storm. This underground building was about nine feet wide by twelve long.

While dark gray clouds were blocking the blue sky, it started to rain and I could see many birds flying and looking for refuge. The atmosphere was getting more and more gloomy and the wind was getting stronger.

—Monche!— Mami called Papi.

—We have to take my mother inside the *tormentera* first.

She was talking about Eufemia, my maternal grandmother. She was sick in bed because of her senyl decay and we had to lay her down on a small bed.

The storm and its effects lasted for two or three days. I still do not know how we could fit three families inside the *tormentera:* the Riveras, the Merced, and our family.

During the tropical storm, I was taking a look among those who were standing by the door and I could see how the wind was blowing away our house roof. I also saw our cow "Ojinegra" tied up to a pole and firmly standing before the wind. I looked at her feeling powerless to offer any help. I could not see her wide black eyes, but I could observe her tight body and legs while resisting the strong force of the wind. There she was, showing that nature, with all its rage, with all its power, was not going to separate her from the family that had taken care of her for a long time and which she had fed with milk. No, not even the rain or the wind could win against *Ojinegra.* Her cattle strength was impressive. She was a champion. Bravo!

I was glad for the endurance of *Ojinegra,* but I felt sad when I saw the big mango tree falling to one side. Nevertheless, being there, and having lost many leaves, its roots kept growing towards the bowels of the earth and kept bearing fruits for a long time and we still could go up its branches enjoying the mango's sweetness.

After the winds stopped, we came out to see a strange world. Many trees were missing. There were many leaves, branches, pieces of wood and zinc swept away from roofs and thrown everywhere, and dead chickens that did not survive the heavy rains. Some houses had been raised in the air and blown up completely. I had the feeling that nature, for which I felt so attracted being a countryside child, was helplessly crying. And I was also crying.

A few days before the storm, Paquita's baby girl had passed away. After a few months, she suffered chronic diarrhea and vomiting. She could not survive and died at Fajardo's District Hospital. The viewing was at my grandparent's home. The baby girl was beautiful and healthy. She had long black hair. Her eyes were jet black.

During the storm, the coffin had to be kept inside the patchouli made *tormentera* and carried to the city's cemetery an hour away. Men had to use machetes and axes to make their way through four kilometers full of fallen trees. According to my brother Juan, who was part of the group, the tomb was full of water and they had to force the coffin down since it was floating like an infant arch.

The dining room from the Manuel Surillo elementary school opened its doors to serve free breakfast and lunch for all those lacking food. They served soda crackers, cheese, ham, canned fruits, and milk, (white or with peanut butter).

After a while, Papi dedicated time to rebuild the house and it was ready in a few days. School started classes and life continued.

THE SURFACE OF MY ADOLESCENCE

During this time I started to feel weird symptoms in my body. I felt like my head was swelling. Tickles ran all over me. I could not lay down, sit, or stand without feeling these symptoms. When I was in bed, I felt like fine sand over the sheets. This made me get up in a semi-conscious state and I used to lay down at any place in the house at night. I remember one day that I woke up inside a cardboard box full of clothes.

Mami took me to some doctors to be examined and I remember that the prognosis was sleepwalking syndrome due to a hit on the back of my head.

There was no sexual education in my family. We could not talk or ask about sex. It was taboo. I believe this was an avoidance for not having adequate knowledge to explain changes in our body, licit or illicit relations, birth control, and other taboos that prevented an open dialogue between parents and children. What a difference between these years and the present!

I do not know how a magazine named "*Luz*" became handy. Its content was sexual orientation including topics like sexual men and women anatomy, men and women orgasm, homosexuality, oral sex, questions and answers on many other topics. All this awoke my interest in knowing the unknown. This magazine was very explicit on information and illustrations. I had to hide when reading it to avoid being reprimanded by my parents. Besides this information, it was unavoidable to listen to my peer's versions about sex.

—Guys, I had a very good night!

This was one of my friend's comments before getting into all the details of a sexual experience with a friend or neighbor.

My infant stripped window smells like castile soap, tropical fruits, ripe *mamey*. It does not have flowers. It has seeds from the flamboyant and carob's acorn, *peronías*, and *camándulas*.

Chapter 2

A-E-I-O-U
THE DONKEY KNOWS BETTER THAN YOU

I started elementary school in 1950, in Manuel Surillo School of *Barrio* Mariana, Humacao, Puerto Rico. I used to walk a distance of about four kilometers to get to school. My brother Flor started the same year. His new name is Rubén, after changing it for personal reasons, which I respect. Even though he was older than me, my parents decided to start school at the same time supposedly to stay together. Parents' protective philosophy that we had to respect.

Being in the same school and the same grade, there was a contest sponsored by the Fire Department to promote the prevention of fires. I decided to participate with my brother as well. We had to paint scenes showing how to prevent fires at home. My older brother, Gregorio, or Goyito as we usually called him, took the role of the tutor to help us with designs, perspectives, and colors to be used. After days and hours of work, we had the projects finished. We both did an amazing job under a brother's expertise.

When the day for announcing the winner arrived, they said that both works were excellent, but they had to select only one, and that one was my brother's project. I felt a wave of deep anger, not against my brother, but those sponsoring the contest. My thoughts, which were focused on everything we could do to prevent fires, turned into an opposite perspective, and I can confess that for not receiving the recognition, I wished everything was burned up; my project, my watercolors I had used, and the homes of those who sponsored the contest including themselves. I promised myself not to participate in any other fire prevention contest. After a few years, this experience made me enjoy the moments when my father was burning up the farm bushes, and while the flames were rising on top of the trees with the rage of a firestorm consuming everything, I felt an immense pleasure like a pyromaniac.

On another occasion, there was an announcement that some scholarships were to be given to students with high grades. It was going to be a payment for fifty dollars once a year from the government of Puerto Rico. I had high grades as well as my brother, but they decided to give only one scholarship per household. And that only one was Rubén, my brother. What a way to discourage an excellent student! I wished I did not have a brother in the same school with the same grades.

Another announcement was made: a pair of brand new shoes for fifty cents. They were the first quality long-lasting shoes. I paid fifty cents and got the shoes, but pride took the place of necessity on my brother.

—I will not wear fifty-cent shoes—he said defiantly.

—Those are cheap shoes!—he declared, determined not to wear shoes that affected his identity.

My parents did not make him buy the shoes. I believe they had to buy a new pair of shoes for him, but I, the last born of the family, the *guajino,* had to accept them. And I did. The *chambones* were black and I had to match them with everything else I wore. In the beginning, I felt that their weight pulled me down to the ground. I wore them year after year. When there was a hole in the soles, I took them to the shoemaker in town where they replaced the soles or the heels to make them last another year.

My first-grade teacher, Miss Rivas, was very pretty. She was tall, white, and slender. Among those interesting moments that we had in class, the one that I was anxiously expecting to happen was when she pulled out a big red book from the drawer with big cursive letters on the front cover: *Canta conmigo.* This moment happened every afternoon at the last thirty minutes of the lessons. Miss. Rivas, with her crystal-clear perfect rhythm voice, broke the routine of the "ma-me mi-mo-mu", (the donkey knows better than you, we said after this to celebrate), and we glorified the *Coquí* song…

> "El coquí, el coquí a mí me encanta,
> Es tan lindo el cantar del coquí,
> Por las noches al ir a acostarme,
> Me adormece cantando así:
> Co-quí, co-quí, co-quí-quí-quí-quí,
> Co-quí, co-quí, co-quí, quí, quí, quí",

> "The coquí, the coquí, I love the coquí,
> Its song is so sweet,
> When I go to sleep at night,
> It makes me sleep singing like this".

…Or the sing-song voice of a well-shaped Puerto Rican bird.

> —Pajarito blanco, verde y amarillo,
> ¿De qué es tu nido? Dime, por favor.
> —Mi nido es de pajas, en él vivo yo,
> ¿Quieres que te cante mi dulce canción?
> Pues escucha niño, así canto yo…

—White, green, and yellow little bird,
What is your nest made of? Tell me, please.
—My nest is made of dry grass and I live in it.
Do you want me to sing my sweet song for you?
Then, listen, little child, this is how I sing…

At this moment we started to whistle the words,
¿Quieres que te cante mi dulce canción?
Do you want me to sing my sweet song for you?
Or the song that exalted the productivity of the mango tree.
"Subamos, amigos, al bosque subamos,
Y presto subamos al rico mangó, al rico mangó.
El árbol que ofrece la fruta bendita,
La más exquisita que el hombre soñó, que el hombre soñó."

Let's climb my friends, let's climb to the forest
And quickly climb the delicious mango, the delicious mango.
The tree that offers the blessed fruit,
The most exquisite fruit that men dreamed about,
That man dreamed about.

I believe that these moments I enjoyed singing at an early age prepared me for participating in cantatas and musicals organized by my son, Titon.

My first-grade teacher loved the countryside life so much that one day she left us alone in the classroom and made a trip to a nearby stream to fish *guábaras*. This is a crustacean that looks like a shrimp, but with tentacles instead of legs. They are dark brown and very elusive. They prefer to stay camouflaged between the rocks with the dry leaves carried by the water.

There was an accident in the classroom while the teacher was out. It is said that "when the cat's away, the mouse will play", and the little "mice " started, not to play, but to fight. During the quarrel, one of the students pushed William, my neighbor, and he ended up hitting one of the columns of the building. Unfortunately, William's forehead made direct contact with the column opening a one-inch deep injury. There was a lot of blood and we called the *Comedor's* employees for help. Eventually, they informed the teacher. I noticed a change in her face when she arrived. The calm, quiet, happy, smiling teacher that I saw before, now looked worried, hesitant, mad, and ready as an executioner to apply the punishment to the student who interrupted her trip to the stream. I can not explain why she did not punish the student who pushed my friend. She hit William, my friend, with a ruler right on his forehead close to the injury. The events after this incident stayed wooly in my mind, but I can affirm that they changed the way I perceived my teacher.

When it was time for lunch, we ran toward the *Comedor* to make an Indian file. A good glass of milk was waiting for us. It was powdered milk dissolved in water. Peanut butter was added sometimes. We had to drink it before lunch. Meals were diverse: rice, vegetables, canned meat, beans, fruits, and eggs. I enjoyed eating yellow rice with soybeans. Desserts were always included: grapefruit wedges preserves, guava paste, crushed pineapple with small pieces of yellow cheese, dry prunes in syrup, or sliced peaches. Doña Ana, the one in charge of supervising, was constantly walking around and saying,

—Here I am again guys. Let's see how you "clean" those trays by eating everything. You can not leave without eating it all—she shouted with emphasis.

If any student was so bold as to leave the vegetables on the tray, *Doña Ana* would say,

—Go back and eat them!

And we had to eat them.

My aunt, Marcola, was one of the employees at the *Comedor*. She was my father's sister and we used to call her *Tía Corina*. She was of low height. She was nice to me. One day, during the *recreo,* I approached the *Comedor* and saw her next to Doña Victoria Burgos, another cook. She was peeling potatoes. My aunt guessed that I was very hungry.

—Héctor, do you want a potato?

—Of course, aunt!

She gave me an already peeled big potato. It was a little hot and I started to blow it to get it cool. At that very moment, the teacher rang the bell telling us that it was time to return to the classroom. I did not want to throw the potato away. The rest of the students were heading to the classroom and there I was trying to eat my potato. I had eaten half of it and I was reluctant to abandon such delicious tuber. I wide opened my mouth and put it inside, but I noticed that it was still hot and made my tears flow. When I entered the classroom, the teacher asked me if I was crying. I had to tell her what happened. There were not any major problems or consequences neither for my lateness nor for swallowing a hot potato. There was only a bitter throat and a happy stomach.

Wrongdoings among students were unavoidable. One day, while I was waiting in line to have lunch, some students informed the teacher, Miss Rosario, who was in charge of allowing five students at a time, that I was cutting the line.

—Miss Rosario, Hector is *colao*—some of them affirmed and the rest agreed by nodding their heads.
—Oh, yes? So Héctor is *colao*? Then Héctor will go to the end of the line—, she commanded.
—*Misi,* I am not *colao na'.* That is a lie—I said.

—You are going to the end of the line right now!

I was so convinced that I was not *colao* and I felt so bitter with what I described as an infant rage and decided to leave the line and not have lunch. Instead, I headed towards the teacher's open classroom, took a piece of chalk and I wrote the following on the blackboard.

"Miss Rosario has a frog's mouth and a witch's hair."

After a while, some students saw what I wrote and they told Ramiro Santana, who was the teacher in charge.

—Are you all sure that Héctor wrote that?—he was asking.

—I don't think so, because Héctor is a well-educated kid and he would never do that.

The issue stopped and no one ever knew who did it. I was satisfied with my revenge.

Children from the countryside used to walk barefooted on many occasions, being exposed to certain diseases. The government of Puerto Rico set once a year for all those students living in rural areas to go back home after taking some medications administered in schools. One of them was the *salsosa,* the name given to this chilling laxative. That day, I wished it never came, we did not have breakfast and we had to bring a glass and a peeled orange. This fruit was eaten after taking the liquid to mitigate its strong flavor. The glass was halfway filled and we were forced to drink that terrible laxative that felt like something obtained from hell. It had a mix of flavors: alcohol, *retama,* and Alka-seltzer. Perhaps, this is why I can not swallow the last one. It gives me flash-backs.

We could not eat solids during the whole day except at sunset when they served us *sopa de leche,* which was white rice boiled and cooked in milk.

A few hours later, after drinking the medication, we started to feel the effects of the laxative. We called this moment to be in *carreritas* because of the frequency and speed we had going to the latrine due to diarrhea. It was the body's reaction while eliminating parasites and bacteria.

In this school, named Manuel Surillo, honoring his compromise to build it, I studied for eight years. Manuel Surillo was the owner of many farms and he used to grow a kind of grass for the cattle that we called *pangola.* Don Manuel was a greedy old man with an unpleasant personality. He exploited the young guys from the neighborhood to work on his farm and paid them seven dollars a week after being exposed to the sun, rain, ants, and exhaustion. Nevertheless, he had contributed with his money for the construction of a two-classroom concrete building for the education of children from the neighborhood during the primary school years.

I was in fifth grade when the cinnamon color skin of Ramonita drew me close to her. We exchanged little notes with our names written on hearts: Héctor and Ramonita. Afterward, we sent each other letters with love phrases. This friendship increased day by day for about four years. When I was in intermediate and high school, I was interested in some other girls like Lucy, Hilda, Eva, and Myrna.

One school year that I enjoyed was when I was in sixth grade. Mr. Lebrón was my teacher. We had our first excursion that year. We visited the famous *El Yunque* and *Playa de Luquillo.* The experience of climbing El Yunque was impressive. There was a narrow path between the trees leading to the peak of the mountain. I was part of the group that wanted to get up there first. When we arrived at *Los Picachos,* as they called this area identifying the highest mountains, we felt like champions. The view from there was unrivaled. We were able to see the fog formations moving below our level. When the air was clear, the greenery of trees was so intense that it looked like a huge paintbrush saturated in green watercolors had brushed them. The different tones of the sky blue were trying to peek, but the fog did not allow the sky to take a look at the vastness of El Yunque. It only allowed the beat of the *coquí* music and the students' happy expressions while they were looking ecstatic at the so close view of the sky and trying to gain their breath after being so tired while climbing. They were saying:

—How beautiful!
—We are very high!
—Look at the clouds as they move!
—Throwdown a rock!
—Do not get too close to the edge!
—Mister Lebrón, William said that a piece of ice fell on him!

Everybody laughed out loud at Williams' words and this anecdote lasted long among us after the trip.

Going down from the mountain, we stopped at *Playa de Luquillo,* a very famous beach on the eastern coast. As we did not have a bathing suit, we soak our feet and legs in the water allowing it to caress them.

Mr. Lebrón, who organized the trip, was very tall and had dark skin. He was assigned to a rented house to teach his classes. It was thirty minutes away from the main school building. We had to go across a stream to get there.

This teacher had a lover in *Mariana II.* On many occasions, he trusted me and my brother to carry his folio with the lesson plans and the key to open the classroom to get the students inside while he was going to be late for having a good time with his lover.

My seventh-grade teacher was Agapito López. He was very dedicated while teaching, but at the same time, he was friendly with the students. He also had an impeccable way of dressing.

Two additional classrooms were built to include the first eighth-grade students. Students who had already registered for studying that grade at the intermediate school Juan Ponce de León in Humacao were told to return to Manuel Surillo school. Most of them did. My brother Rubén did not want to return and he stayed in the city. It was our first year studying in different schools.

My eighth-grade teacher was very nice. I admired him because he recognized my interest in the education field.

—Héctor, do you want to help me?

—Of course, mister! How do you want me to help you?

—Write this material on the board so the students may write it down in their notebooks.

This was the beginning of many other tasks that he designated for me to do and I complied with great interest.

One of my classmates was Zory. Her complete name was Zoraida Castro. She was my aunt Marcola's granddaughter. Zory was a beautiful girl. Her deep black eyes contrasted with the whiteness of her skin. She had a beautiful smile. Her thick and long hair was shaped into a braid. I was one of her admirers. I felt a platonic love for her. What prevented a declaration of love for her was that I was informed that she was my cousin and that cousins do not fall in love. But it was enough for me to see her every day, being next to her, laughing with her, enjoying a school day next to a girl with so much beauty.

To be ironic, Zory got pregnant by a cousin and it was not me. The rumor was spread like gunpowder. When she was taken to a doctor for an exam, she was still a *señorita.*

I studied my ninth grade in Juan Ponce de León intermediate school. I remember my Spanish teacher, Mrs. Cabrera. She was medium tall, she wore glasses and she had a very protruding belly. She had a unique methodical way of teaching.

She was well known for her project *Costumbres y tradiciones,* from the novel *La hermana San*

Sulpicio. This assignment was to find customs and traditions in this literary work. The more of them, the better the grade.

I had a friend, Efraín Guadalupe, a pastor's son, who had taken the class before and he helped me by adding more information to my list. The day I had to hand in my work arrived, and I felt very satisfied for having found so many costumes and traditions.

Each student had to sit on a designated chair positioned next to the teacher's desk. Mrs. Cabrera started to browse the works page by page with the scrutineer eyes she had and getting ready to deliver her judgment: a successful or failed work of a student. She called on a student's name that was immediately before mine on the register.

—Bring me your work!
—Yes, teacher, here it is.

Her eyes behind the glasses were moving with an extraordinary speed while browsing each page of the work. We could only hear the noise of the papers while being pressed on the lower right corner. We could hear the students buzzing through the windows while talking and laughing in the park next to the building. They were waiting for the ring to start a class. Once in a while, we could hear the car's horns on the street. The student next to the teacher was nervous and looked like guessing what was going to happen. And she guessed right.

—Why did you write just a few?
—I did not find many—she said.
—Then, your grade can not be higher than a C.

After this, my project came before the teacher. She browsed the pages and I observed that the teacher paid attention to the last page of each section. She then told the student that was before me:

—Look, if you had done it like del Valle's, your grade would have been an A also. This project is complete.

And I said to myself,

—Thank you, Efraín!

Although I felt happy for my grade, I also felt a deep pity for that student, because it was not appropriate for the teacher to compare two works from different students in front of the class.

My high school years were extraordinary. Miss Torres, eventually Mrs. Torres was my English teacher in tenth grade. We knew about her wedding date and the administration assigned a temporary teacher during our teacher's absence. When she returned from her honeymoon her husband brought her to school on a pickup. They always kissed each other. Some students made funny comments:

—Look how she walks with her legs wide open.

It was not true. It was an indirect way of saying that she had lost her virginity.

Miss Antonia López de Victoria was my Spanish teacher in eleventh grade. She had a very special aristocratic look. She took care of her physical aspect in a particular way. She was not tall, but she had a very slender body and was famous for wearing nice collars.

One of her assignments was to memorize the famous Sigismund's (Segismundo) monologue from the book *La vida es sueño*.

Sigismund was the son of King Basilius who was warned by a prophecy that one day his son would rise against him in rebellion, and so he had the child locked up in a tower from where he said his famous monologue.

I remember when a student asked this teacher for her first name.

—It is not your business—was the teacher's answer when she felt trapped between her decision of not saying her first name and a group of students that were willing to hear a different answer.

Everybody turned their heads toward Doris, the one who asked the question, and there was a mumbling among the students like saying, why did you ask?

It was in this school where I met an ugly and skinny girl. I still do not know why I kept her as my girlfriend for such a long time, because she was skinny to a superlative degree. She also had acne. Her nose was carrying two nostrils that seemed to inhale all the air around them, and when she spoke with emotion, those nostrils were wide open.

Her name was Hilda Diaz and she was the daughter of a custodial that worked in the vocational school. Her family lived in Barrio Buena Vista. Hilda did not have lunch with us in the school's cafeteria. She belonged to the group of students that believed the lunch served in the cafeteria was not good. She rather walked to a relative's house in the same city to have regular food instead of a well-balanced lunch. Hilda was sure to return to the school park located between the elementary and intermediate schools. Of course, she would find me there waiting for her.

She was coming with fresh makeup. The recently applied powder was highlighted on her cheeks. Her thin lips looked like the underscore key of my computer. Once in a while, she had tiny pimples on her face. I smelled a soft perfume as I approached her. A great unease was noticeable when she was talking. She was a little apprehensive, because, as she told me, she did not want to be caught by surprise by her father while talking to me. That prevented me from kissing her. We used to hold hands instead.

Hilda and I were, as I call it, intermittent friends. Sometimes we broke up our relationship for insignificant reasons and then, we started from zero again.

My school's stripped window has canary flowers and poppies, and the scented flowers are always alive. This window was made with branches from a weeping willow.

My parents: Ramón and Saturnina

Chapter 3

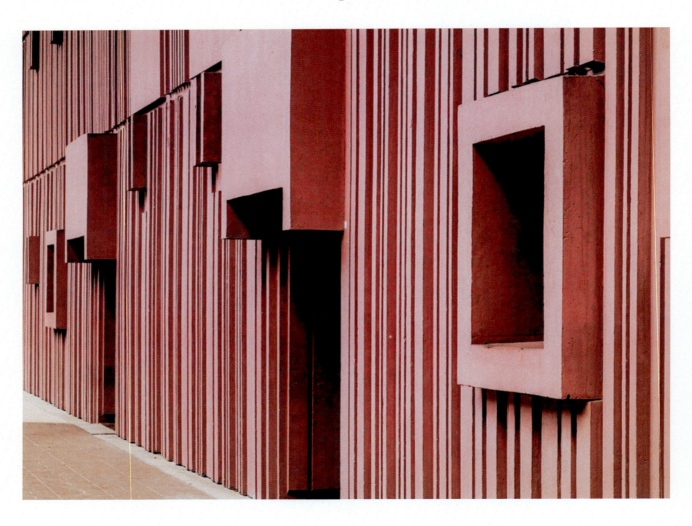

MY MOM LOVES ME

Mami. They used to call her Doña Tunila. Even my sister Virginia called her Tuna. Her first name was Saturnina. The third daughter was named after her. After she got married, she changed it for Nina, maybe for having a name of so many letters, or for resounding issues. Maybe she did not like the idea of being linked to Saturn, the planet, or with a name taken from *Almanaque Bristol.*

Mami left deep footprints in my personality. Today I believe that for being the last born in the family and for having what others said "baby face," I was the one closer to my mother.

Papi was never interested in his children's matters He never spoke about sex with us, however, Mom did it in a very disguised way. Papi was an excellent provider, but he was not the kind of father that we could approach to share our private matters. Mom, at least, listened, and advised us within her intellectual limitations and using practical terms like, "Don't you have sex until you marry."

Doña Tunila was of medium height, dark skin, happy eyes, and with an easy constant smile. When she smiled, there was a contrast between her white teeth and the cinnamon color of her skin. We could see a golden tooth among the others.

She was an excellent cook, but she did not cook every day. She assigned this work to the firstborn, Alicia, who, after being separated from her husband, never got married again. She returned home until she died.

It was Mom who got up every Saturday and Sunday early in the morning to go to *Plaza del Mercado* in the city of Humacao. She could buy fresh meat and vegetables. I remember that the meat she bought in great quantities was beef, so she made a stew with whole potatoes every other Sunday. This was my predilection for food. At the very moment Mom entered the kitchen, it was like a diva taking control of the culinary art.

The kitchen building was separated from the house. It was a *dos aguas* shaped as carpenters used to call all buildings that were like an inverted "V." It had two doors: one was used as the main entrance, and the other one was to the left. Inside, and on the right side, there was a rustic wooden chest made by my father. It had many shelves. It was the pantry holding the family foods: ground coffee inside an empty *Klim* or *Denia* powder milk can, sugar in another can, rice inside empty soda crackers can. Some were kept inside the same purchased paper bags, like beans or chickpeas. The moment that the pantry was opened, we sensed the mix of aromas coming from the coffee, cinnamon, oregano, and other condiments kept inside.

In the background, there was the *fogón* designed by my father. It was a wall-to-wall table with two parallel iron rails with crossing steel rods. There was a metal sheet over the table to prevent a fire. Pieces of wood were placed in the center and impregnated with kerosene gas to light up the fire that would cook white rice, beans stewed with white salted bacon, potatoes and squash, meats, spaghetti, breadfruit, and so many other foods for feeding a family of thirteen members. There were three meals: breakfast, lunch, and supper.

To light up the fire, we had to go to the farm to get the wood.

—Mami!—shouted Alicia—We have no more wood.
—Then, send someone to get it—said Mami.
—I told them, but no one wants to go.
—What? Wait up!

And we knew the meaning of that "Wait up! It meant that if we did not comply with Alicia's command, Mami was going to punish us. Before she approached, we already had the machete and rope in hand to go, cut the wood, and tighten it up with a rope as soon as possible.

Looking for wood was a chore we had to do before the existing wood was finished. This was a whole adventure walking through the farm and looking for the appropriate dry wood, cutting it into pieces, and packing it.

—When you look for wood, avoid bringing it from the *cenizo* tree—reminded Mami. This was a tree with a straight thick trunk full of pines. It was not easy to light up its wood and there was a lot of smoke during its combustion. We had to be very selective about doing this chore.

Another family task was to bring water for cooking. We did not have the drinking water system installed in our neighborhood and we depended on a stream or *pozo* as we called it. It was located at the end of a slope on our farm. We had to go down a narrow path with a *latón* which had a rope tightened up around it to carry it easily.

The water from the well tasted different from the rainwater because it was filtered through some rocks. On some occasions, there was a *buruquena* coming out of a hole. We used to bring it home, boil it in salty water and eat it.

Looking for wood as well as bringing water from the well were necessary tasks for the preparation of the three daily meals.

A typical breakfast included freshly brewed coffee. These grains were from our neighbor's farm Don Martín, toasted on earthenware by Alicia, and grounded in a *molinillo*. This last chore was rotative and done by the last three brothers. A nontypical breakfast included oatmeal or cornmeal. My favorite breakfast was an empty can full of sweetened coffee with soaked pieces of crackers which I enjoyed eating using a spoon. These crackers were called *rompe-pechos* for their thickness. They were sold at the Don Sabás store.

The lunch, served at twelve, always included *viandas* from the same farm: yams, breadfruit, and *malangas*. These were harvested from the swamp. My father told me how to get them using a machete. I had to cut the top section off and plant it again to have a new plant. Codfish, onion rings, and oil were mixed as a side dish.

Dinner included white rice with stewed red beans. A pair of fried eggs, sausages, or corned beef was included. I remember that after all the rice was served for the whole family, part of it remained stuck to the bottom of the pan. We called it *pegao*. My sister Alicia unstuck it with a spoon and served it with the bean broth. It was delicious. On occasions, she shaped it like a ball with her hands and gave it to us.

I used to sit in the *batey* with my brothers Juan and Rubén to enjoy our pegao succulent meal. While our palate was being satisfied with the greasy crispy rice, we made some comments:

—This is delicious!
—I wish we always have rice, so we'll always have pegao.
—Of course, because when they cook soups, we will not have pegao.

During this moment the three family pets were next to us: Miso, (a cat), Tintán, and Puppy (two dogs). Tintán was white and very aggressive. These dogs were always watching us so we could share some pegao with them. We liked to throw them small pieces so they could catch them up in the air. Sometimes we fooled them by looking at how they opened and closed their mouths with the only movement of our hand. Today, I believe we committed canine cruelty.

The sunset was painting some colorful shades. First, it was the orange that slowly turned into coral red over horizontal lines on the clouds. While the evening languished and the sun surrendered to the pressure of darkness that was beginning to lay down its immense black evening gown over the field, we were surrounded by the metallic prelude of the *coquí* that would turn into a twelve hours concert without interlude. Up in the air, bats started their nocturnal flight. We were eating *pegao*, they were eating insects.

When darkness succeeded in driving away from the ornament of the different shades that decorated our countryside sky, we rushed to get inside our house to sleep, not before a story narration like "Ali Baba" was narrated, or the sinister and mysterious one that says at the end, "...and give me the meat that you ate." Another story was the one with a song: "Brother, do not touch me, nor let me without a touch..."

We did not have electricity until the beginning of the fifties. We used kerosene lanterns. The trembling light of the lantern made some shapes over the zinc and wood walls. Using the light and our hands, we projected images of a dog and a rabbit. There was a strongly burned kerosene smell all over the house. The *toldos* were installed around our beds to keep us safe from mosquito bites, not before spraying a mosquito repellent in the air using a pump. We called this "flea,"

It was a joyful celebration when we saw the workers in charge of installing the electric cable poles and how they went house by house installing the connections for the light bulbs and other electric household artifacts. After it was completed, my mother decided to buy an electric refrigerator from Casillas Furniture located in the city of Humacao. This refrigerator took the place of the one we had, which was made of isolated aluminum with an opening on top to store a huge ice block and a door in front for keeping some foods from spoiling.

The electric service changed the country's life. We started with a light bulb in each room, a non-battery radio, a refrigerator, and a record player. Don Fermín, the owner of a neighborhood grocery store, was the first one to buy a television. We knew about it and we asked permission to visit and watch it.

—Mami, can we go and watch television at Don Fermin's house?— we begged.

—Yes, you may go, but do not come late nor bother the family.

And there we were. A group of children from the neighborhood sitting on the floor, amazed by the magic of the television programs. The cinema world was opening before our eyes and we enjoyed it, indeed. We came back home around ten o'clock.

I liked to see Mom cooking. She was very detailed, especially when preparing some particular dishes: beef stew with whole potatoes and a cup of pure grape juice, spaghettis, *majarete, arroz con dulce,* and the dessert I used to prepare following her style, green papaya preserve. Her secret, according to her, was to cut the pieces into half-inch thick and six-inch-long and soak them in ash water. This allows the cooked papaya to get a special texture: a little crispy on the outside and soft on the inside. Today, when I prepared this dessert, I used baking powder or bicarbonate powder to substitute the ash and I got the same texture.

The most exciting and intense moment was when the papaya started to soften. The whole kitchen had a smell transformation. It was a place with a smoke smell, but it permeated with a mix of aromas from the cinnamon and the caramel melted brown sugar. This ambiance transported me to an unimaginable world.

—Mami, is it ready?—I asked many times.

—Not yet. It will be ready when the syrup gets sticky—she affirmed.

The making of the *majarete* was another fascinating moment. This dessert was made especially for Christmas time. It was cooked in a big cast iron pan because it was going to be for the whole family including our neighbors: the Riveras and the Merced. During its preparation, Mami had to stir it constantly to prevent the formation of lumps. I waited until the end because after storing it on deep aluminum plates, Mami gave me what was left in the bottom of the pan. I ate it with great fruition. It was still warm and it tasted better than the rest. It seemed to be that the combined flavors of the ground rice, sugar, coconut milk, and vanilla were concentrated in the bottom of the big pan.

My mother's heroic character came to light when my father was diagnosed with tuberculosis. Papi started to cough frequently and I saw him throwing big amounts of phlegm. Mami insisted on a visit to see Doctor Franceschini at the Municipal Hospital, but Papi was very hesitant and stubborn. Later, he decided on the doctor's visit and he received the sad news: he tested positive. He had to be hospitalized for a long time in a hospital in Cayey. During that time, Mami was taking care of her mom, Eufemia, who was in bed for her senile decay waiting for the eternal embrace.

During this time, my sister Nina was studying Secretarial Science at a private college in the city of Humacao. Her studies and all the family expenses were covered by public charities. In other words, every Saturday, Mami took me with her to those places where the sugar cane workers were paid. She was standing in front of the line and every time a man got paid, Mami would beg to say:

—Please, help me. My husband is in the hospital and my mother is sick in bed.

(Chinese proverb)

Some gave a quarter, half a dollar, a dollar. Others turned their heads ignoring the plea. It was at this exact moment that I felt sorry for my mother. Feeling her resignation when she did not receive any money, I also felt a deep rejection for those who did not feel compassion for a needy woman who surrendered her pride to support a big family during a desperate situation. On the other hand, I think that many of them were in a similar situation thinking that giving a dollar away was a great risk for them for not being able to support their own needs.

When we got home in the evening, I helped Mami to count the money. This was going to be used to buy the weekly groceries and our school travel expenses.

At the beginning of the week, Mami was searching for the next paying place, so next Saturday we will go through the same routine.

According to Mom, she got married or was forced to get married at the age of fifteen. It was not a fancy wedding like the ones we have today. It was not planned ahead of time like a contemporary one. It was very common for the groom to "steal" the bride. They agreed and at a certain time at night, he would get near her parent's home and would grab her and run away. The next day they were both in the groom's parent's home. Neighbors were talking about it the next day.

—The one who ran away with her boyfriend was *fulana*—they used to say.

Although Mami did not like Papi at the beginning, his conqueror spirit overcame the rejection of her loved one.

Before marrying Mom, Papi had another woman. I do not know if he legally married her or not. Her name was Marcola. They had two children: Petra and Rafael. I saw her many times in my neighborhood. Marcola went nuts, maybe because Papi left her to marry my mother. Marcola was constantly walking up and down the road in front of my house. She was always scruffy, wearing rags, and saying incoherent words. Her lower eyelid was torn. Some neighbors felt sorry and offered her some food. She looked neglected by her son Rafael who lived nearby in a small two-bedroom concrete house where he procreated and raised thirteen children.

Petra, my step-sister, had some bitterness for my mother. I found it when Petra traveled to my house from New York City where she lived for many years. She affirmed that my mother had taken away Marcola's husband.

Mami's stripped window is pink and it smells like *alcoholado*, camphor, and beef stew with bay leaves and whole potatoes. It has the sweetness of grape juice.

Family members

First born Alicia

Chapter 4

THE DOZEN-PLUS ONE, WHERE ONE CAN EAT, THIRTEEN CAN EAT

My parents raised thirteen children. I was the last one. Out of thirteen, two of them passed away at an early age. I was told that their names were Goyita, the baby girl, and Gamaliel, the baby boy.

Being part of numerous families is interesting. We have the opportunity to see the wide presence of our ancestors' genes: diversity in the skin and eye colors, hair color and texture, height, and other physical traits inherited from our ancestors. Such diversity was manifested in my brothers and sisters.

Let's start with Alicia, the oldest. She went to live with Santos as a couple. Her honeymoon did not last long because my mother interrupted her romance when she went to their house to inform her husband that Alicia would not be the ideal wife for him for being mentally unfit and could not comply with the responsibilities as a wife. Her husband agreed and Alicia returned to my house. Afterward, on some encounters they had, my sister would ask him for money.

Alicia did all the cooking for the entire week. She prepared the three meals for the family except on Saturdays and Sundays when Mom was in charge. Alicia was very talented when brewing coffee in the morning. She used a white piece of cloth to transfer the coffee that was boiling in water and at the end, she used to press the cloth to get the extract of the just brewed coffee. Then, she kept the wet coffee powder into a container to make a second coffee in the afternoon that was called *borras*. This second coffee did not have the same flavor as the one made in the morning, but it relieved the effect of not having drunk coffee for twelve hours.

While Alicia was making coffee, Papi was milking *Ojinegra,* our cow. He extracted a lot of milk and then he made the calf suck the udder again to get more milk. This second one was very creamy and it was reserved for Papi. Alicia added sugar and milk to the coffee and served it inside an open can that was emptied of its contents.

At eleven, Alicia was peeling the breadfruits or yams for lunch. There was a particular yam from a plant called *maracas.* Its flowers had a hard red round seed called *peronías* which was used to make the sound inside a *maraca,* a percussion instrument.

In the afternoon, Alicia always cooked white rice in a *caldero,* a big iron cast pan. She also cooked beans or chickpeas that were soaked in water the day before. She also seasoned any available meat for frying.

Another chore assigned to Alicia was washing the clothes. I remember helping her carry the packs of clothes on many occasions. It usually took the whole day to finish this work. She used a big rectangular blue soap bar. She used to hit each piece of cloth with a flat piece of wood against a rock. There were other ladies from the neighborhood with her and they were always gossiping about their neighbors.

—Doña Manuela gets jealous of me with Chilí, her husband—Alicia commented.

—Really?—asked another lady—Why?

—She says that I keep watching him from my house, and it is not true. That lady is a gossiper. Do you think that I will fall in love with that old man?

—And what does she tell you?—asked a lady

—She insults me saying, "You, daughter of a b-," and then, she tells me to stop looking at her husband.

—And what is your answer?

—What am I going to say? I tell her that I am not looking at anybody, not even her husband, but she keeps talking and talking. She looks like having a motormouth.

—Yes, she is a blabbermouth. What you have to do is talk to your mother, so she can straighten her up.

—She has insulted my mother, too.

—Has she insulted Doña Tunila? Your mother is a saint!

—Just like that, but Mami does not insult her. Mami tells her, "The Lord rebukes you, Satan!" and she gets angrier.

—Tell me something, Alicia. Don't you like Ignacio?

—Impossible! I still love Santos, my former husband. Sometimes, I find him on the road and I ask him for money.

—And does he give you the money?

—Of course, he does! He does not give me much money, but I will take whatever he gives me. He is a good man.

And they kept talking and talking for a long time and they only stopped to get up from the rock where they were sitting to spread the soapy clothes over other rocks to allow the sunlight to help get the dirt out. Afterward, they returned to the same routine of washing and gossiping.

In the meantime, we were playing in the ponds enjoying the river's fresh and cool water while it was sliding through our innocent and tender bodies. We could see the presence of birds singing and flying from tree to tree, while the bamboo trees were dancing from side to side and making a special soft sound. It was like an orchestra of sounds from the river, the ladies hitting the rocks, the birds singing, our movements splashing the water, and the dancing bamboos. The *pomarrosa trees* offered their shadows and sometimes, they dropped a fresh, juicy, and sweet fruit which was dragged by the river. We swam to grab it very fast and enjoyed its rich honey sweetness.

Alicia was very protective of her brothers and sisters. If my parents reprimanded anyone, Alicia was acting like a whole "defendant's lawyer."

Papi's character was like Alicia's: very strong. One day, something tragic happened. Papi was reprimanding Mami for getting home late from church and the "defendant's lawyer" came into action.

—This is not the appropriate time to get home—said Papi with emphasis and raising his voice.

—I was talking with Virginia—Mami said.

—The conversation could have taken place on another occasion—argued Papi.

—Calm down, Monche— said Mami trying to relax him.

—Yes, he must calm down, because Mami was not doing anything wrong—affirmed Alicia.

—You keep quiet!— yelled Papi.

—I am not going to keep quiet!—answered Alicia.

At this moment, Papi walked toward Alicia and Mami followed him and told him to be careful about what he was going to do, but Mami got there late. Papi had caught Alicia by her neck and was trying to choke her. Mami hit his hands to get them loose. The next day Alicia was taken to the hospital, due to the blood marks on her neck. I ignore what story Mami told the doctor about it.

Virginia was born after Alicia. She married Eduardo Oyola, or Chito, his nickname. They had the same number of children that my parents had: thirteen. When she gave birth to Efraín or Palín, she contracted tuberculosis. Mami took care of Palín, who as a grandchild, had some privileges that I never had. One of them was a brand new bicycle that Papi bought for him.

Virginia used to call Mami, Tuna. When they finished attending church, they stayed in front of the building talking about different topics. I heard their conversations. They talked about everybody.

Ismael or Monchito was born after Virginia. He married Ramonita or Monchita. He was a barber in the city of Humacao. He was very generous with us. He told us to put grass under the bed during the day before King's Day. In the morning we found toy cars that he purchased for us. He was the "King" that placed the cars.

He always told me:

—Héctor, you are hairy and broke.

I answered:

—Well, give me a haircut and a penny.

Monchito liked a beautiful blond girl from the neighborhood. Her name was María Esther. I saw them together on many occasions. I imagine she was his lover. When he was older, he passed away from complications of diabetes. He went through some amputations.

Gregorio or Goyito was next in line. He was very dedicated in school. First, he had a Bachelor's Degree from the University of Puerto Rico and then, a Master's Degree from the University of Pennsylvania. He had a beautiful girlfriend from the same university. Her name was Judith. He did not marry her due to her drinking habits, as he said. He married Basilisa or Sisa, our neighbor's daughter.

While he was single, there were two girls from the neighborhood that liked him. I remember seeing him in the river with them. They were laughing and having fun with my brother. I tried to hide to avoid being seen.

Narciso o Siso was next. He was a very dedicated and responsible hard worker. He always worked in the same place: a factory called "Textron". He loved motorcycles. He had his own to travel to the city. He spent many hours on the maintenance of his motorcycle. He also could play the accordion, and sometimes he gave us a concert on the house balcony. He had a premature death due to chronic prostatic cancer.

Nina, one of my sisters, studied at a private college to become a secretary. Tito, a pastor's son, fell in love with her. Tito was very attracted to many girls from church, but he decided on my sister and used to visit her in my house.

Years later, Nina married another pastor's son, GiddelMartínez, who loved her truly. In the meantime, Tito did not have a healthy marriage with Aida, whom he met in New York City, and ended up in a divorce.

Daniel. The military. After his discharge, he married a blond blue-eyed girl: María Elena. They had three boys.

Ana was the blond girl of the family. She had white skin, a shaped nose, and full lips. She also ended up being divorced.

Juan was the oldest of the last three boys. His name was Juan Bautista. Flor, (Rubén, today), and myself were the last ones. Juan was very ingenious. He seemed to have an answer to every question. He did not have a happy marriage ending in divorce.

Rubén was next to the last one. He was very talented in mathematics. He achieved his college degree and worked for the government of Puerto Rico.

I hated going with Rubén to catch the avocados that my father threw from up the tree into a sack. Sometimes we failed and the avocado broke into pieces. I found this work to be so boring. My father used to sell these avocados for family support.

Two events reunited the family: Mother's Day and Christmas Eve. For the first, each one brought a gift for Mom. Colorful clear papers like red, green, yellow, blue, and orange were used to wrap the gifts. The dining table was reserved to display all the gifts. We also took a picture of the family having Mom in the center. In the afternoon, we had rice with pigeon peas, *gandinga,* yams, and roasted pork.

The pig to be roasted had been raised for a long time. Papi used to kill it the day before, holding it by four people with a stake on its neck. Hot water was poured over the pig to soften the skin and shave all the hair. It looked very pale like the bacon used for *chicharrones.* After removing all the internal parts of the body, they rinsed it with water and vinegar, added the necessary condiments to marinate, and tied it up on a pole until the next day at five o'clock in the morning. At this time, Papi already had two sticks forming a "Y" which were used to hold the two extremes of the pole where they had the pig. The lighted wooden charcoal was in place between the sticks and the long roasting process began. Papi boiled some oil with annatto seeds to brush the skin of the pork, giving a reddish color to it. We could hear the comments of those in charge of turning the roasting pig.

—Do it fast to prevent it from burning!
—Move those charcoal pieces, so the roasting is even!
—Mmm...that pork smells good!
—The tail is for me!

Some of them approached and took some small parts of the roasted meat to keep repeating the "Mmmm…" and licked their fingers. The emanated aroma from the combination of the meat being roasted, the charcoal being sprinkled by the fat from the meat, and the smoke that retained the essence of an almost roasted pork, embraced the whole place and traveled on the wings of a mid-day soft warm breeze reaching open doors and windows of the nearby homes. Our neighbors knew that Don Monche and Doña Tunila were going to share the roasted pork with them.

The big family stripped window has many mouths, hands, and arms. It is inclined to the left side and we could see the sun through it. It discharges aromas from *yerba buena, claveles de muertos,* white jasmines, coffee from a *colador, and* freshly roasted pork.

Teaching in Hillcrest High School

My first graduating class from El Cabrito

Chapter 5

GOING UP *"THE CABRITO"* HILL AND DOWN HIGHLAND AVENUE

I was twenty years old and just graduated from the University of Puerto Rico where I studied for two years under a program named Normal from the Pedagogy Faculty. I was at the school superintendent's office, whose name was Mr. Vázquez. He had offered this teaching position to many candidates who were qualified, but after knowing that the school was in a very secluded location like *"El Cabrito"*, they refused the offer.

This was a challenge for me. At this moment, I reflected that if the son of Monche and Tunila had walked a long distance to get to school every day, and that he could get to the top of a mango tree to feel the strength of the wind when it made the branches to dance while he was up there, and if he went uphill and downhill looking for *fresas,* guavas, *pajuiles, mameyes,* and many other fruits, challenging the difficulties involved, why he shouldn't accept the great opportunity to go up the "royal" road that will lead him to the sacred place of *El Cabrito* school?

I accepted the challenge. At that moment my life was marked by one of the most meaningful experiences that would last as a live memory of what I could do to enrich the lives of some countryside children.

I took the ride to the city and from there to El Cabrito. I got off the public car and started to walk through the royal road that would lead me to the school. Some people going down the hill greeted me with a smile. I went across a shallow stream avoiding contact with the water. I could see the abundant vegetation on both sides of the dirt road. There was a constant sound from the variety of birds from the trees up until I arrived. I even felt welcomed by the Puerto Rican wildlife.

I finally got there after a thirty-five-minute walk and the students were waiting for me.

There were four students: two girls: Sofía and Vivian, and two boys, Fidel and José. These last two were brothers. They lived in *EL Cabrito,* located in the mountains of Mariana.

Mistrust and shyness were merged in their looks, but a soft expression of happiness was perceived in front of the newly neophyte teacher that just arrived.

And there I was, the guajino, the babyface, the last born to Ramon and Tunila, the one who, at an early age, started to dream of becoming a teacher, the *campesino, the jíbaro,* the one who, as a child, had probably the same experiences of these four: playing outside when it was raining while being naked, taking care of the cattle, sinking our feet in the mud, sliding down the hill on a *yagua* as a sleigh, climbing up the trees, looking at the stars at night, enjoying the sweetness of the mango, the *fresas*, the guavas, the cashew apples, lemons, *chinas,* June plums, *maricaos, cherimoyas,* and so many tropical fruits from Puerto Rico.

This was the beginning of my educational career journey. I started with a few humble students in a modest classroom on a steep location surrounded by the typical trees and bushes, mangos, laurel, acacia, bamboo, and oaks.

—Good morning, guys!—I told them, trying to get a response.

They did not answer. The greeting got lost on the stream echo that winded nearby. The youngest was barricaded behind his brother trying to protect himself from the strange look. They all were wearing not quality clothes, but they looked clean and well pressed. One of the girls looked like wearing a dress from her older sister, for its sleeves extended well below her elbows. She had an unhealthy look missing the natural pink color of her age. Her eyes were like a clear sky without clouds.

—How are you guys?—I kept saying and trying to get an answer from these children who were still with a mix of astonishment, surprise, and shyness.

—My name is Mr del Valle, and I am here to be your teacher—I affirmed.

After a while, I got closer to the children and they took a few steps back as they felt the presence of a stranger. I did not hesitate on my approach and extended my hand to José, the tallest one. He had very white skin, blue eyes, and well combed blond hair. He had a hesitant smile while having one hand in his pocket and used the other one to move Fidel, who kept barricaded behind him.

—Fine, we will have time to shake hands. Let's get into the classroom—I told them.

José was holding my briefcase while I was getting the classroom key handed to me by the superintendent.

It was a single classroom made of concrete. It was not painted. There was only a front door and four double windows on the opposite side. The concrete floor looked rough and covered with dust. The building was located on the side of a hill and to get to the door you had to walk through a long concrete stair that started a few feet from a stream. When I opened the windows, there was a breeze that dissipated the humidity odor enclosed inside during the vacation time and it was changed by a pleasant clay and wildflower smell from the front yard of a house next to the classroom.

I scoped the space: classroom, knowledge temple, two blackboards, students desks, teacher's desk. Everything was showing simplicity that matched very well with those children that, although already inside the classroom, kept silent and only smiled at each other while having furtive and concealed looks for the just arriving teacher.

The moment was interrupted by a sweet and clear voice heard from the main entrance.

—Mr. Del Valle, welcome to El Cabrito! I know you will like it here.

It was Doña Felícita who was entering the classroom. She was in charge of the cafeteria where the children would have lunch daily. She was about forty years old with a well-shaped face, a little shy, but very helpful with the students and with the only school teacher.

—I hope so—I responded.

—Where are you from, Doña Felícita?

—From Buena Vista—she said.

—And you come from so far away?

—Of course! There was no other available place for me to work.

It seemed like we both shared the same situation of being sent here because others refused to. At this moment I felt like being assigned to what others rejected. It was like the popular saying, "taking leftovers".

But in reality, it was not like this. There were no "leftovers". It was not the worst. That was a tiny corner of the world with human beings, parents, children, brothers, whole families, and neighbors that deserved a good teacher to accept the sacrifice—like theirs—being that all these people sacrificed time and efforts to achieve a goal: the construction of a single classroom for their children, so they could have an appropriate place to receive instruction near their homes.

At that precise moment, I considered myself a good teacher.

A good teacher was in charge of changing four walls into the most highly sacred campus. The words, the numbers, the concepts, the ideas, the songs, were going to take a special, unique, and different character surrounded by a country foreground with the metallic sound of the stream, the song of the *pitirre,* exalted on top of the palm tree mast, the lilting *reinita* hiding in the *cariaquillo,* the whiny turtle dove with its incomparable "U-u!, U!, U!, U!, the polyvalent hymn of the *ruiseñor* with its multiple variations. All of them will witness the shaping of habits, skills, abilities, knowledge, and attitudes that are necessary to achieve many goals in the fresh and innocent minds of children like José, Fidel, Vivian, and Sofía.

As time passed, the group increased to twelve.

That year was difficult for the students. Some were affected by different illnesses preventing their attendance. Sometimes, when there was heavy rain, some of them couldn't get to school. A few of them had to wait hours for the rain to stop.

During heavy rainy days, there were strong water currents carrying mud and dirt that flooded the stream located between the school and the area where the students' homes were. I could see the students from the classroom door and made some signals like transit police leading vehicles in a dangerous place. The big difference was that they were human beings who had challenged the heavy rain and the slippery dirt roads to get to a place that meant so much for them. There they were standing and carrying umbrellas very close to the riverside that was like talking to them and saying:

—You can not come across. My strength is powerful. You should return.

But they did not return. Their persistence was superior, and after a few hours, they could cross with no harm. They came escorted by their parents who facilitated their arrival at school.

During these days the learning process was irregular, but I took advantage and explained the effects of rain on human beings, the flowers, and on the wildlife. Many students' questions were answered.

One afternoon we received the sad news. Rafael, a student who recently arrived, was riding a horse. It was his favorite hobby. We saw him riding his brownish horse many times at a fast speed. One day, he fell during a ride and broke his leg. He was taken to the hospital and returned home with a cast. For this reason, he could not attend school for a while. When I found out about this, I made a home visit to see him.

I could see the humble house from a hill. Its roof and walls were made of zinc sheets. It was a small house. It was *dos aguas* style. It had a front door and windows on both sides. It was a very common country house. On that afternoon, the sun was reflecting its light upon the trees, reclining their shadows on the house which was showing the front side only while the rest was partially hidden among the shadows and other trees around.

Rafael's father came out of the house into the *batey* upon my arrival and greeted me with exhilaration.

—Oh, look who is here! Rafael, here is your teacher!

—Good afternoon—I greeted him.

—May you have a good afternoon!—answered him and immediately he made me go up the wooden stairs and into the house living room.

They had a simple set of furniture made of straw. There was a blend of two smells in the air: a recently lighted off cigar, and the smell of beans being cooked from the kitchen. Shy pale sunlight was filtering through a window in a hesitant way avoiding the interruption of the shack interior's twilight. Carnation's fragrances from the front yard were mixed with the clear notes of the pitirre standing on top of a royal palm. A former white hammock, now of cream color for its constant use, was hanging from two corners at the center of the living room. Rafael was resting on it,

His well-defined eyes by his abundant eyebrows had a sudden shine. He had shaggy hair when he stood up from the hammock.

—You came to stay—affirmed the father, meaning that I was going to be the country school teacher forever.

—We never had a home teacher's visit. You are the first one visiting us. Would you like to have *un poquito 'e café?*

I nodded.

What a genuine way for the Puerto Rican countryman to offer what he has to the visitor! It comes out very spontaneous, natural, unconditional.

While I was waiting for the coffee I started a conversation with Rafael and his father. The mother, who had stayed quiet, went across the living room into the kitchen to make the coffee.

We talked about Rafael, about how he fell from the horse, about family children, about the farm, about their poverty, and the hope they had to see their children graduating.

I admired the fact that these parents who did not have the opportunity to study for higher learning grades for any reason are now compromised to help their children to overcome their limitations.

After having the black and aromatic coffee we finished our conversation, I expressed my gratitude for their hospitality, and promised that I would return another day. I felt the satisfaction of leaving the family full of happiness and hope.

After a year in this school, I was able to celebrate the graduation of the sixth-grade class having some students in the Honor Roll.

The next year I was transferred to another school and I lost contact with my students.

After working as a teacher for two years, I decided to return to the University of Puerto Rico to complete my studies and obtain a Bachelor's Degree in Secondary Education. I graduated in December 1967. During the same month, Uncle Sam hired me for military service.

I returned to the education system from Puerto Rico after being discharged from the Army in 1969. The following year, I got married and worked in Puerto Rico until 1984. I then decided to move to New York City. I worked in Manhattan, and later in Highland High School in Queens. In this school, I met excellent colleagues. There was one whom I considered my closer coworker: Doctor Roberto Montesinos y Barrio. He was a very wise Spanish teacher from Colombia who also loved to teach philosophy and real life. He was a motivational mentor who was constantly persuading his students to achieve high. I believe that many students were able to change their lives radically because of Roberto's advice.

In 2005, I decided to retire from my professional career. I started the process according to my will: a retirement while I was enjoying good health; and this was the right moment.

Nevertheless, the transition did not happen as I had planned. It took me some time to adapt to the new life of being retired. I had to stop getting up early in the morning. The routine of being in front of five groups of students while teaching came to an end. My mind transported me to those moments when I was surrounded by groups of students who were shaping their futures. I could not get rid of fifteen, twenty, or more youngsters that were telling me about their need to master their native language. They were always in my mind.

After many years, my students are present, like looking at me through nocturnal "windows" in my dreams. I could feel the anxiety of those who struggled to succeed, of those who felt rejected for their sexual preference, of those who did not have many friends, of those who felt the effects of being shy, of those who were verbally or physically abused by a relative, of those who missed their native land and culture, of those who found too hard learning a foreign language, of those who did not enjoy a good and nutritious breakfast, of those who were not heard by their parents during difficult moments. Many of them succeeded; a few gave up. One girl committed suicide.

Being without an audience of about a hundred students that attended my classes to receive learning that would enable them to survive in a complicated world, I had enough time to ponder about my job as a professor.

Did I accomplish the mission for which I was born? Was I the exemplary professor to whom my students looked up to emulate? Did I walk the extra mile? Did I go beyond the call of duty? Did I commit the "omission sin" by not doing what I was supposed to do for which I studied? To be honest, the answer to these questions is an absolute yes, except for the last one which requires a no, because I believe I accomplished all my goals as a teacher.

Being a teacher goes beyond the simple task of transmitting knowledge. It should include the understanding of human growth and development. This is part of the teaching curriculum, unfortunately, not all those who are involved will implement it. It made me feel uncomfortable when a coworker commented on the context of the extra help that foreign students need.

—I was prepared to become a professor, not a counselor.

At this moment I remembered that one of my subjects during my college studies was "The teacher as a counselor." My coworker was wrong. I was right.

The performance of a holistic teaching profession can not avoid the counselor function. I am not referring to the formal systematic counseling of a professional, but to those spontaneous moments that may arise during our teaching mission and even after school.

This function will mark the students' lives in such a way that they will remember us, not only as their teachers but as human beings, too. Nowadays, some graduates use the teaching job as a "springboard" to get into a different working position.

This stripped window is gray like a cloudy afternoon before a rainstorm and has some green shades like the mango tree leaves.

At the age of twenty-five as a member of the US Army

Chapter 6

EATING FROM SMALL BOXES ON THE OTHER SIDE OF THE WORLD

I was the only one in my family that was recruited by the US Armed Forces. I have a brother, Daniel, who volunteered for service. I remember when I turned eighteen, I registered for mandatory selective service. It was Mr. Ramiro Santana, from Mariana, who filled out my application. This professor had a low height, fleshy lips, and a very strong articulated voice. He was a teacher at Manuel Surillo elementary school. We attended this school during our primary studies. I believe he stayed single for the time I met him. He also had a special dedication to his job performance. He was a true teacher by calling. When you looked at him on the implementation of his job, he transmitted the passion felt when you do something you like.

Following his instructions, I registered as a conscientious objector for military service. This meant that I did not believe in killing another human being, but I could serve our nation in another way not including bloodshed.

In the last semester of my studies towards my bachelor's degree, I received orders to take the United States Armed Forces admission tests. I submitted a deferral to finish my studies which was approved. By January 1968, I joined the US Army. I traveled from Buchanan to North Carolina for induction and from there to Fort Sam Houston, Texas, to take the basic training including classes to become a combat medic without the use of weapons.

During my stay in San Antonio, I had the opportunity to visit the world fair, celebrated in this city in 1968. I used to go downtown with my friends and spent long hours visiting the different pavilions while tasting different foods from the countries represented in the fair. One of my favorites was a dessert made with corn mill from the Philippines. In May, I was assigned to work in a hospital in Fort Ord, California. Being there, my job was to take care of patients who had upper respiratory infections. This base was located in Monterrey.

Monterey is a city on California's rugged central coast, on the shores of the Pacific Ocean. This city was immortalized by novelist John Steinbeck, born in Salinas, California. He grew up in a fertile agricultural valley about twenty-five miles from the Pacific Coast. Today, it is a popular strip of gift shops, seafood restaurants, and bars in converted factories. At the time I visited Monterey, I was not aware that I was stepping on his native city. What a privilege for me!

Being here, we could feel the salty impregnated ocean breeze and we could hear the constant cries of the seagulls while hovering over the water and looking for food. At the floating pier, you could walk a good distance to enjoy the great noisy spectacle of the sea lions blending with the black rocks.

On many occasions, I traveled from Monterey to Carmel, a small city located in the mountains. From there we could see the majesty of the ocean and the painting exhibits displayed on the streets by local painters.

My work at the hospital followed a routine, except for changing my schedule. Some days I was sent to other wards to take care of other patients who needed care of their physical functions. One night I had to watch a soldier who took an undetermined number of pills and was intoxicated. I had to keep him awake so he could not go into shock. I could sense how fragile a human being could get caused by depression. This soldier was not even in his twenties. He might have taken the decision motivated by the separation from his family or for any other reason, He thought that killing himself was the best solution.

Sometimes I reflect on the process of people who host thoughts that are conducive to life self-rejection. Is it the pile of experiences by which, instead of feeling valued by friends or relatives, they feel saturated by curses about their failed lives, their defects, their limitations, their differences, their sexual orientation? Is it a deviation from the values and principles of society, the family, the church, making them feel like they are wrongly doing things that were not expected, but doing their will guided by instinct, by their passions, and not by the "compass" they received? Is it by not being able to go against all this to keep a firm stand, so they may value their lives themselves?

While working in this hospital I met Mrs. Davis. She was a civilian nurse. She was around her forties. She was short, had a strong voice, and was very talkative. She told me she had a daughter who was still single and had talked to her about me. Her daughter asked her if I was handsome. Mrs. Davis said that I looked fine. I never told her that I was interested in her daughter since I did not want to have the disappointment of seeing a girl who might have been biased and then tell me that I did not like her. I believe it is better to meet a girl by incidence and not by influence.

I preferred to work during the midnight shift at the hospital, so I could sleep seven hours and still had the afternoon free. Another benefit was that for having this schedule for a month, I could enjoy a four-day weekend. During one of these days, I had the opportunity to visit San Francisco. This city has its peculiarities.

The Golden Gate Bridge is a suspension bridge spanning the Golden Gate, the one-mile wide (1.6 km) strait connecting San Francisco Bay and the Pacific Ocean. It was declared one of the Wonders of the Modern World by the American Society of Civil Engineers. It is also the most suicide site in the world. It is very impressive. Looking at it from the pier, its reddish color is highlighted over a blue sky canvas.

I traveled to the Fisherman's Wharf using the electric trolley. This place is attractive to people who enjoy eating seafood. There were various merchants with high chairs and tables in front of their shops. They had a furnace for boiling, roasting, or frying the seafood depending on the client's requests: lobsters, shrimps, fish, clams, octopus, mussels, and others. We could have a great feast while enjoying the sea breeze and the aromas of the food being cooked. The island of Sausalito could be seen in the distance. A tourism boat was approaching to disembark its enthusiastic tourists. All this was happening at the beat of the restless seagull rustic concert that kept hovering over the sea, over the returning fishing boats, and near us to fight over a piece of food we may have thrown. I tried to identify which seagull was similar to the character in the short novel, "Juan Salvador Gaviota", but none of them had the same character traits.

After I enjoyed this banquet, I traveled to the island of Sausalito. The mist was floating in the air like an immense transparent silk bride gown. It was more intense as we moved closer to the island. It gave me a sense of peace which was only interrupted by the boat motor noise. We could see other boats coming and going. Some travelers waved their hands. We responded. While the pier was distant, Sausalito was welcoming us. I enjoyed my stay on this island for its nice weather.

I returned to the base after having a great weekend in San Francisco. A few days later, I received a phone call while I was working at the hospital.

—Are you Héctor del Valle?—asked the person.

—Yes, I am Hector del Valle—I affirmed immediately.

—You have orders for Vietnam. You will depart in December. Report to the central office to pick up your orders.

I felt that my life was going to take a drastic change. I knew that this was going to happen, but I always tried to ignore it for being afraid of dying on a war front. It was a feeling of resignation and opposition at the same time. Besides, being in the army, I had to obey orders that were just, but I had the right to appeal to those that were against my beliefs.

I applied to obtain a compassionate reassignment for the states of New Jersey or New York due to my mother's critical condition. I wanted to be closer to her in case of death. The petition was denied and I was given a month's vacation to spend in Puerto Rico before going to Vietnam. To make things worse, I had an outbreak of chickenpox during the same days before my trip to Puerto Rico and during my stay on the island.

My farewell day arrived. I wished it never did. I decided not to inform my mother about my destination. She would have an adverse reaction due to her heart condition. I was saying goodbye to my family, which for them it was a "see you later". Deeply inside of me, I was struggling with the pessimistic idea of not returning alive, but in a coffin. I was saying goodbye to my relatives including my mother who had sacrificed herself taking care of the big family and making sure they all ate three meals a day. I could not hold my tears while saying goodbye to those around me and to the barrio where I spent the first twenty-five years of my life picking up pieces of wood from its forests, carrying water from its streams that emerged from its insides and ran under the shadows of the *guamás* and pomarrosas. Saying goodbye to the hills that I used to slide on a *yagua,* to the orange color sunsets that painted an impressive heavenly world on the canvas of the multiform clouds, and the paintbrush of the half-hearted and timid sun while sliding through the soft cloud silhouettes leaving behind a whole natural artwork with which I felt captivated on the synesthesia of its imagery.

I was afraid of no longer enjoying these personal experiences of a nature that saw me when I was born, that saw me growing up, playing around, getting soaked of its unlimited offerings, of its generous attributes, for this *guajino,* the youngest of Don Monche and Tunila, stepping on a foreign rice field ground of people threatened by death, of a sky not covered by amazing sunsets on a fraction of one thousand five hundred Puerto Rican miles, but a gray sky covered by the mortar and artillery smoke, of the human blood and flesh burned by napalm, the viscous fuel that causes terrible burns. On the contrary, I would see sunsets without twilights, sunrises without dawns, days when the twenty-four hours would vanish among the routines of the war fields, of the ambushed attacks, of the friends that would lose the fight under the deadly AK-47 shootings, of the booby traps, and the mortar attacks.

I left. Still crying. I traveled to *Isla Verde's International Airport.* From here to New Orleans, to Los Angeles, to Washington state, and then to Vietnam on a nocturnal twelve hours stopover flight. We arrived at Da Nang Base early in the morning on December twenty-third. When I got out of the plane, the country "slapped" me on my face with the heat. My skin could not resist the extreme heat of this country. At a distance, we could hear the strong noise of artillery being shot at the enemy forces. As the noise diminished, we started to feel the strong bacon smell coming from the Mess Hall where the three meals were cooked and served for the soldiers. Later, I was transferred to Cu Chi and assigned to work in a medical dispensary.

I was welcomed by Sergeant Manning and assigned to Company C, Twelve Battalion of the Twenty-Fifth Infantry Division. I went into the barrack, the shack where I was going to sleep. It was made of wood and zinc. It had doors in front and back. It was divided into room sections with a hallway in the center. There was a building behind it with a big water container on top to be used as a shower. Next to it, was another small hovel or latrine with a seat and a hole on it. It had a container to receive the human waste. This container was removed weekly to burn the waste with gasoline. When this was done, the air was impregnated with a stink for the combinations of gasoline, urine, and …(opening the window a little), of shit.

I could not sleep well that night. First, because the cot was very uncomfortable and also for the constant artillery noise nearby. I thought about what I had left behind: a very cushioned bed, a calmed sleeping time, the certainty that the next day I was going to be alive. Everything changed in the last month. I was experiencing profound insecurity, knowing that there was a high chance of being killed into pieces.

Sergeant Manning approached me one day.

—How do you feel, Héctor? Are you fine? —he asked as he was working with some papers.

—I think I am fine—I nervously answered.

But I was not fine. I was still struggling with the question of why I was in this country.

Mr. Manning kept talking.

—This is war. You are going to live it, no one is going to talk to you about it. You must follow my instructions for the possibility of being sent to the front combat line. Many of my medics did not return alive. Some were killed either by the bullets or by the mines. If there is a shooting, you hit the ground immediately and barricade yourself behind an object: a rock, a trunk, whatever is close to you. If you see a Vietnamese sign indicating mined fields, you must walk extremely carefully. If you step on a mine, you could lose your extremities or your life.

The *regalón* was shaking from head to toe at this moment, indeed. The son of Tunila and Ramón was sweating cold without being tired. My life was in front of the death's door and my heartbeat increased to about one hundred per minute,

—But remember, if you follow my instructions you will have better chances of surviving— trying to calm me down after he notices my nervousness.

But he could not. A fatalist thought caught my mind. My mind was transported to my native town, to my *barrio,* to those places I used to walk and run when I was a child. To the farm where I used to look for wood to light up the *fogón* for cooking. To the hammock where I slept quietly in the living room. To the abundant lilting river that slipped through the sand mountains ornamented with rocks and making the cold refreshing current clash against them and embracing my young growing body under the bamboo shadows, while the force of the wind made them friction as they were extending their arms over the water like a protective arch. My mind took me to the grassland where I laid down facing up while looking for the constellations during the *coquí* and crickets saturated music nights. It also took me to the moments when I talked to *Ojinegra,* the gentle family cow. Finally, it took me to the moment when I stamped my signature during my mandatory selective service registration.

I wanted to backtrack the time, but I could not. The frustration was so intense, that I returned to the barrack, I hid my head under a pillow, and I cried like a vulnerable child full of fear. I needed a hug from someone to calm my anxiety. Perhaps, my mother's hug so she may speak words of courage and security with her sweet and tender voice. I needed a hug from someone, it did not matter from whom at that moment, but I could not find it.

The next day, while I was at the dispensary's pharmacy, I heard the noise of the front door when it opened and closed with a hard hit. I also heard the voice of the soldier who entered and started a conversation with Sergeant Manning. He was talking with anguish.

—Sergeant, I am coming to give you the bad news—he said.

—What happened?—asked the sergeant.

—The platoon medic stepped on a mine and died instantly. We need to send a new medic.

And I was next in line. I was going to be the next medic. There were no doubts. The time for PFC (Private First Class) Del Valle had come to take the place of the fallen medic. I was not going to be in Cu Chi base where I was almost secured because the perimeter was far. I was going to be inside another perimeter closer to the enemy.

—Del Valle, get ready to depart tomorrow—commanded Sergeant Manning.

—Yes, sir!—I answered without hesitation.

The next day I was sent in a convoy to a small base in a town called Trang Bang. From here I was going to go out to the field as a combat medic with a platoon. I was given the necessary medical equipment to take care of all the combatants' emergencies in the front line. It had gauzes of all sizes, salt tablets to prevent losing minerals for the extreme heat, morphine shots to mitigate the acute pain when losing an extremity or suffering severe injuries, scissors, and other additional equipment. I was not carrying a gun because of my status as a conscientious objector.

Our first incursion was by helicopter. We were split into groups while waiting to be lifted. After fifteen minutes seven helicopters landed making a V-shaped position. I was impressed when we boarded these helicopters that had no doors on the side, so the deployment of troops would be as fast as possible. While we were flying we could see the symmetrical large flatlands planted with rice in water channels. We also hover over dense woods with the possibility of being shot by the enemy forces of the Viet Cong or by North Vietnam troops.

While we were preparing to descend to a point where we could make contact with the enemy forces, we got out and ran to look for protection. At this moment I started to hear some shots that almost blew my ears. I thought that the son of Tunila was going to die at that moment. But it did not happen. These shots were made by the soldiers from inside the helicopter to protect us from enemy fire while we were slipping under the bushes.

My term at the front line as a medic lasted for six months only. We went into ambushes day and night. Along with our equipment, we used to carry a small brown box with the lunch that we were going to eat in the front line. Sometimes we had heavy rains and we were water-soaked while sleeping outside. On certain occasions, I could see how some powerless families were looking with rapt attention at how the army tanks were destroying their rice plants, the watermelons, the vegetables. I could imagine all the rage inside of them toward us when they saw that their time-consuming labor for the feeding of their children was ruined in minutes.

There were places where only the mother with her small children was found. Their husbands had escaped before the American troops arrived and some hid in tunnels avoiding the betrayal of the enemy forces.

An experience during our ambushes in the frontline made me feel very uncomfortable and somehow an inside wailing being part of a group of soldiers who under the orders of a captain and a lieutenant did not show respect for human dignity.

We arrived at a small village to set up a security perimeter to spend the night and to wait for a large company of enemy forces that were nearby and were ready to start an attack. There were two shacks made of straw next to each other with two mothers and their respective small children. A questioning started with the help of a translator to find out where their husbands were. Both mothers refused to give information while repeating: "I do not know" in Vietnamese. Before their negative attitude, one soldier, under the approval of the lieutenant and the captain, started to rip the clothes of one of the ladies. He started with the blouse while two other soldiers pushed her to the ground while one was holding up her arms. Her breast was exposed and her face was full of shame for the terrible humiliation. It was not enough to strip her clothes, push her to the ground and expose her breast allowing the rest of the soldiers to watch her like a whole circus. The same soldier took a knife and brought it near her nipples threatening to cut them if she did not cooperate. But she kept saying: "Tói khóng biét" meaning " I do not know." This scene was being observed by the other mother and by all their heartbroken children.

But the soldier did not give up. He took her pants and her underwear off exposing her private parts. This time he started to remove some pubic hair with the knife while the mother started screaming, but always saying the same words.

Finally, they decided to let her go with her children still crying, her clothes stripped, and full of shame. Later, another soldier discovered her husband hiding in underground tunnels covered with recently cut grass. They were taken out and questioned. To get information from them, they hit them with wet towels making deep bruises on their backs, but they also kept saying that they did not know anything. They were taken out by helicopter as prisoners of war.

That night we were expecting a big attack from a North VietNam Army Division. We had to dig a trench for our protection. I remember that after being inside the trench I decided to come out of it and lay down on a bunch of dry grass that was nearby. Around midnight, I did not feel secure being there, so I decided to go back to the trench. Wise decision! The next morning after the big attack I discovered that a mortar bullet had made a big hole exactly where I was laying down, right on top of the dry grass. I believe God was watching over me.

This experience, or better saying, nightmare, made me ask for a consult with the Chaplain so he could help me get out of the front lines. While I was talking to him he kept silent with no reaction. His answer was;

—You have a short time left in the front line, why don't you wait for a little more?

And that "little more" could mean my death at any moment. I had to resign myself. Each day we returned from the field, I thanked God for keeping me alive.

There was a bridge over a dry river near the base. Almost every day we found mines on the dirt road and they decided to create a plan to watch for the gap between the time that those watching the bridge left and the time when the next platoon left in an ambush, which was around seven o'clock. It was a two-hour gap and the Viet Cong knew it and decided to install the mines on the road for the next day. The plan was to have the area protected for those two hours while the other platoon left the base. The first time we did this was with my platoon. The area was almost completely flat with a few terrain elevations without any area for barricades.

There we were complying with our orders. Suddenly, we spotted two Viet Cong soldiers walking through the bridge at a fast pace. We called base for immediate mortar attacks on them. The mortar attack started, but at the same time, the other platoon was near the area already and when they saw us, they called for mortar again believing that we were Viet Cong soldiers. We were afraid of being hit by the mortars from our people if it wasn't for the immediate identification of both groups.

Another scenario that made a strong impact on me was when our platoon leader stepped on a mine. This happened about twenty meters away from me. The shout for help came after that. I was told to walk towards him carefully due to the probability of more mines. I walked firmly, but cautiously. When I saw my friend, I had to hold my emotions. His right leg had been damaged by the mine and I could even see some fractured bones and a lot of blood. My duty was to stop the bleeding immediately and prevent him from going into shock. He probably needed an amputation. The first aid helicopter was called and he was evacuated.

One of my Puerto Rican friends was Lugo. We called him like that using his last name. He used to live in Chicago. He was always anxious about something wrong that could happen to him.

—Del Valle, I have heard about what some guys are doing to get out of the frontlines—he told me.

—What are they doing?—I asked.

—They are shooting their feet themselves during an enemy attack.

—Are you planning to do the same?

—I would do it.

And one day he did it. Fortunately, the bullet just touched the tip of his toe without any big injury. I was called to examine him and I decided to clean the area, apply an ointment and a small gauze. He stayed with us without being evacuated. Eventually, while doing a road sweep, he was hit by a "booby trap" grenade which caused him multiple injuries on both legs and he was evacuated.

Later, I was offered to travel to a nearby country for rest and restoration (R&R) for a week. I chose Japan. It was a great trip to this beautiful country. I visited the cities of Yokohama and Tokyo.

I returned to Cu Chi base and shared my experiences with Sergeant Manning.

—I am glad you rested and had a good time—he told me.

—Do you drink, Hector?—he asked me

—No, Sergeant—I answered.

—What? You do not know what you are missing.

—The truth is that I was taught not to drink—I affirmed.

—Then, I will teach you how to drink—he firmly told me.

—I don't think so.

—I want to invite you to a meeting I will have with all the non-commissioned and commissioned officers from our battalion this coming weekend. You are going to have a good time with us—he informed me

—I promise that I will attend, but remember that I don't drink —I told him

—Don't worry, del Valle.

During that night I was offered the opportunity to play a Spanish guitar and to sing any Spanish song. I chose "La Bamba", a well-known song by most people. There was a glass full of coke next to me, but Sergeant Manning started to add small amounts of whisky. The music continued along with the mix from the glass. Everybody was singing with me and we laughed and talked about stories from the war. After a while, I started to fall asleep and at the same time, all my emotions were overflowing. I was aware of what was happening. I decided to go back to the barrack, but I could not stand firm. Sergeant Manning and another officer took me to the barrack where I fell asleep until the next day.

—I told you, del Valle. I would teach you—he told me with a big smile of satisfaction.

And if you think that I continued with this practice, the answer is NO. I only use wine once in a blue moon.

This window is black like the wood charcoal extracted from the *hoguera campestre,* and red like the *cundeamor* fruit. It smells like gunpowder and burned human flesh with bullet holes.

EPILOGUE

ANOTHER NON STRIPPED WINDOW

After I retired from the New York City Education Department in 2005, I decided to change my status as part-time senior pastor to full-time until 2008 when I decided to retire. I sold my condominium and moved to Orlando, Florida in 2010. It was a big change. From a city where we have everything near, to another city where we depend on having a car for transportation to shop around. From a city with a full season change to another with the eternal Summer. I had to make some adaptations from weather to transportation.

I dreamed that if I had to move to Florida, I wanted a house with a swimming pool. This dream came true in 2015 when I purchased a pool house in Winter Park in Seminole County. It has a big backyard where I am implementing my skills as a "farmer". I have banana plants, sweet peppers, pineapples, pigeon peas, okra, a guava tree, a grapevine, and my beautiful passion fruit vine that gives me two harvests a year.

What's ahead? That window is semi-stripped but I have one reserved option that will be revealed soon. For now, it's a secret.

Slammed!

GLOSSARY

¡Adiós Cordera! - A Spanish short story written by Leopoldo Alas. It is a touching story of two children who loved their family cow, like a mother.

Agua de tiempo- It is the water collected in containers when it rains

Alcoholado- Eucalyptus alcohol.

Almanaque Bristol- It was a small booklet with various topics like predictions about the weather, horoscopes, jokes, and advertisements. There was a list of proper names for each day of the week and parents used to pick the one that matched their newborn babies.

Almojábanas- Cornmeal fritters

Árbol Madre- It is a metaphor for the guama tree that grows casting its shadows over the coffee trees like a mother.

Arroz con dulce- A dessert served during Christmas time. It is made of rice, coconut milk, sugar, cinnamon, and ginger.

Barrio- A Spanish-speaking quarter or neighborhood in a city or town

Batey- Name was given to a special plaza around which the Caribbean Taíno built their settlements. It was also the name of the surroundings of the countryside homes.

Bembeteo- It is a rectangular sweet and hard caramel candy.

Benjamín- The last-born of Jacob's thirteen children according to the Bible and the last-born in a family.

Borras- After brewing coffee, they used to re-use the powder for making more coffee.

Brisas del Caribe- A fragrant cologne used as an aftershave.

Buruquena- Is a freshwater crab in streams of Puerto Rico.

Caldero- Traditional cooking pot used for cooking rice and other foods in Puerto Rico. It has different connotations according to the local towns, existing the word "olla" for the same pot.

Camándulas- It has its origin in a rosary with thirty-three counts. It is also named "St Peter's Tears."

Campesino- Country person

Candelarias- In Puerto Rico, bonfires were an accustomed norm for urban and rural Candlemas

Celebration on February 2nd. Everyone gathered a conical pile of burning wood Pieces. Many local Catholics still consider the feast a logical end to the Christmas season.

Canta conmigo - Book "Sing with me."

Cariaquillo -Lantana Camara is a species of flowering plant within the verbena family, native to the American tropics.

Carreritas- It was going to the latrine many times due to diarrhea.

Cazuela- Clay pot

Cenizo(tree)- It is a tree with spines.

Central Ejemplo - One of the many sugar cane mills located in the eastern city of Humacao, PR

Cerezas - Star Gooseberry fruit

Chambones - It was a sarcastic word for the heavy pair of shoes.

Chicharrones - Fried pork meat with skin.

Chinas - Oranges

Chirimoyas- Custard apples

Ciudad Gris - Gray City. The former name was given to the city of Humacao, PR. The new name is City of the Rising Sun.

Claveles de muerto - Dead 's carnations. This flower was displayed on top of the coffins.

Colador - Elongated cone-shaped piece of cloth used to brew the coffee.

Colao'na - Expression that is formed from two words: "colao", a contracted form of "colado" (cutting inline) and "na", contracted form of "nada"(nothing, negative).

Comadrona - In rural areas it was common to call a lady who assisted mothers in delivering the newborn.

Comedor.- School lunchroom

Coquí - A species of frog endemic to Puerto Rico belonging to the family Eleutherodactylidae.The species is named for the loud call the males make at night. This sound serves two purposes. "CO" serves to repel other males and establish territory while the "KEE" serves to attract females.

Corito - A short Christian song.

Costumbres y tradiciones- Custom and traditions

Denia- A powdered milk

Dos aguas - Homestyle built like an inverted "V".

El Cabrito - Literally "The little male goat"

El Pueblito de los Perros - "The Dogs Little Town".

El Yunque - The Caribbean National Forest located in Luquillo, Puerto Rico.

Fajardeña - Native of Fajardo, PR.

Fiambreras - Portable covered dishes used to carry hot meals.

Fogón - Wood cooking fire originally made with three rocks.

Fresas - Puertorican strawberries.

Fulana - It refers to any lady.

Gandinga - A thick Puerto Rican stew made with pig organs as the key ingredient.

Gofio - A typical Puerto Rican sweet made from roasted corn and brown sugar.

Guábaras - Dark color river crustacean of Puerto Rico.

Guajino - The last born from a female pig.

Guamás - Inga Edulis, known as ice cream bean for its sweet flavor and smooth texture of the pulp.

Hoguera campestre - A bonfire used as a celebration

Jácanas - Fruit from the bully tree. It is almost extinct in PR

Jíbaro - Rural Puerto Rican with distinctive dialect and customs.

Klim- A powdered milk

La Hermana San Sulpicio - Sister San Sulpicio. A Spanish novel written by Armando Palacio Valdés.

Latón - A commercial metal big container. It had lard inside to be sold by pounds. When empty, it was used to carry water from the well.

La vida es sueño - Life is a Dream. Play written by Spanish writer Pedro Calderón de la Barca.

Los Picachos - This is a short hike that is along the side spur of the El Yunque Trail, and leads to a stone masonry platform with a 360-degree view vista point.

Luz(Light) - It was a small magazine that included sex education.

Majarete - Puerto Rican rice pudding

Malangas - Starchy root vegetable that grows on damp grounds.

Mamey - Mamey sapote or mamey colorado is an important fruit in PR.

Mampostiales - A shredded coconut, sweetened with brown sugar prepared for a dessert.

Mango tino - A variety of mango fruit with a round shape.

Manuel Méndez Ballester - A Puerto Rican writer who also worked in journalism.

Maraca - A showy flower that resembles an easily recognizable musical instrument is called the maracas. Some people used to dig out its roots for cooking them.

Maricaos - Nance fruits

Molinillo - Coffee grinder

Muchas gracias - Thank you, very much

Ñangotao - Squatting position

Ojinegra - Name of the family cow meaning Black-eyed.

Pajuiles - Cashew fruit. It is considered a forgotten fruit in PR

Pangola - A very thin grass planted for cattle food.

Pegao - Sticky rice from the bottom of a pan.

Peronías -The seeds of the maraca plant. They are shining red with a small black dot and inserted inside the maraca to make the sound.

Pitirre - Gray kingbird

Playa de Luquillo- Luquillo Beach

Plaza del Mercado - Marketplace

Pomarrosas - Rose apple fruit

Pozo - Well

Recreo- Break time for the students to have any outside activity.

Regalón - The last born in a family, like a big gift.

Reinita - The Puerto Rican Amazon (Amazona vittata), is the national bird of Puerto Rico

Retama - It is believed that this flower contains cytisine, a toxic alkaloid

Rompe-pecho - Hard round crackers.

Ruiseñor - Common nightingale

Salsosa - It was a drink used as an antiparasitic.

Sopa de leche - Soup made of rice and milk

Señorita - Miss.

Surillana- Neologism by creation. It comes from the last name of Manuel Surillo, the founder of my elementary school.

Tamarindo - Tamarind is a sour fruit for making drinks.

Terraplén - Plateau

Tiempo muerto - Novel written by Manuel Méndez Ballester. It also refers to the time when there was no more work at the sugar cane mill.

Toldos- Cotton canvas used for protection from mosquito bites.

Tormentera - A reinforced concrete small building to stay safe during a storm or hurricane.

Un poquito'e café - Apocope of "A little bit of coffee", (letter "d" is omitted).

Viandas - This term refers to different meanings according to the country. In Puerto Rico, it is used as yams in general.

Yagua - This is the part that holds a real palm tree leaf to its trunk.

Yerba buena - Spearmint plant

Zafra - The time when the sugar cane mill is in operation.

Printed in the United States
by Baker & Taylor Publisher Services